YOU
DON'T
NEED A
LAWYER!

D0062105

YOU
DON'T
NEED A
LAWYER!

James M. Kramon, Esq.

Library of Congress Cataloging-in-Publication Data is available.

  ISBN-13: 978-0-7611-4038-2
  ISBN-10: 0-7611-4038-7

Cover design Paul Gamarello; book design Patrick Borelli
Cover illustration Robert Dale

The material and information presented in this book are not intended as a substitute for professional legal, accounting, or other advice. In matters requiring such advice, a suitable professional should be consulted. All names and addresses used in this book are purely fictitious, and any resemblance to real names or addresses is coincidental.

Workman books are available at special discounts when purchased in bulk for premiums and sales promotions as well as for fund-raising or educational use. Special editions or book excerpts can also be created to specification. For details, contact the Special Sales Director at the address below.

Workman Publishing Company, Inc.
708 Broadway
New York, NY 10003-9555
www.workman.com

Printed in the U.S.A.

First printing: October 2005
10 9 8 7 6 5 4 3 2 1

To my mother, for teaching me
the value of persistence

Acknowledgments

I am indebted to my literary agent, Julia Lord, for making this book possible. Julia's advice and hard work are deeply appreciated.

My editor, Jennifer Griffin, provided countless important suggestions for improvement. I benefited greatly from her experience and expertise.

My good friends Barbara Dale and John Weiss supported my work on this book from its conception. They provided many important ideas and proofread drafts with a critical eye. I am very grateful for their friendship and efforts.

I could not have completed this book without the tireless assistance of Nancy Sumwalt. She typed, revised, and organized every part of the book. Nancy has the invaluable ability to recognize when I have the mark and lets me know it. Every writer should be so lucky.

CONTENTS

Introduction 1

Think Like a Lawyer 5

The Effective Letter 9

The Letters 37

    GOODS AND SERVICES
    (letters 1–23) 38

    HEALTH CARE
    (letters 24–37) 95

    LIABILITY
    (letters 38–39) 134

    GOVERNMENT AGENCIES
    (letters 40–44) 139

    BANKS, INSURERS, CREDIT CARDS
    (letters 45–57) 154

    CEASE AND DESIST
    (letters 58–60) 182

    COLLECTION
    (letters 61–62) 189

    NEIGHBORS (letters 63–64) 193

    SCHOOLS (letters 65–68) 197

    LANDLORDS (letters 69–70) 207

    EMPLOYERS AND CO-WORKERS
    (letters 71–73) 211

TRAVEL
(letters 74–78) 219

LETTERS IN YOUR DEFENSE
(letters 79–81) 232

SETTLEMENT LETTERS
(letters 82–84) 239

Appendix A 247
A BRIEF GUIDE TO SMALL CLAIMS COURTS

Appendix B 259
FEDERAL AGENCIES

Appendix C 261
STATE AGENCIES

Consumer Protection 261
Independent Review Panels for
   Health Claims Decisions 275
Insurance Commissions 289
Banking Agencies 296
Education Agencies 305
Agencies That Accept Consumer
   Complaints Against Credit Card
   Companies 313
Transportation Agencies 323

Appendix D 329
CREDIT REPORTING AGENCIES

Index 330

Introduction

I t's rough being a consumer these days. Companies we deal with seem indifferent to our needs. Salespeople have abandoned traditional values such as honesty and trust, and most could use a refresher course in basic manners. Fewer and fewer transactions rely on personal relationships as businesses (and government agencies) become bigger and more bureaucratic. When we have questions or complaints about products or services, it's often impossible to get a response, much less a reasonable, courteous one. Gone are the days of the mom and pop shop. Gone is the motto "The Customer Is Always Right." We are not in Grover's Corners anymore.

Many ordinary retailers who would once have been neighbors or friendly acquaintances are now part of multibillion-dollar national or international organizations. We buy cars, clothes, food, furniture, and nearly everything else from nameless, faceless salespeople at companies that sell to millions of other nameless, faceless customers. These businesses have absolutely no interest in our individual satisfaction (although some of them fake it pretty well). Even the smallest businesses that we regularly deal with—perhaps a landlord who owns an apartment building or a service business with a few hundred customers—don't seem inclined to deal with customers who might take up time and money.

I have practiced law for thirty years. My clients have the same problems with retailers, service people, hospitals, airlines, schools, and employers as everyone else. But they deal with them differently: They hire me. And I get responses for them—usually the responses they were hoping for—every time. Is there something special about me? Or about my clients? Honestly, no. The reason lawyers get responses is that we know the right buttons to push. This book won't give you a law degree, but it will teach you how to push those buttons yourself.

Lawyers have three ways of getting their points across to people they are trying to influence: talking, writing letters, and filing lawsuits. Of these, letters are by far the most effective. Talk is cheap, as the saying goes, and in the sorts of situations most people face today, it can take forever to find out the right person to talk to about a particular matter.

The Best Revenge

I have had clients who have wanted to "teach a lesson" to negligent service providers or unscrupulous merchants. They have wanted the culprits to feel shame and guilt over their wrongdoing. I offer you the same advice I give them: Don't. You have no control over other people's consciences. Your goal is simply to get what you deserve. If your HMO is denying you medical treatment, your purpose is to get it to provide that treatment. If your new automobile continues to stall on the highway after three visits to the dealer, your purpose is to get it fixed or replaced. If your bank tries to charge you for money you don't owe, your purpose is to make it relent. This book won't help you change the world, but it will make it easier for you to live in it.

Talk may be useful once a letter gets someone's attention, but it's rarely of any use before that occurs. Lawsuits are time-consuming and expensive. They are a hassle that everyone wants to avoid, and reputable lawyers reserve them for large disputes in which an amicable settlement cannot be reached.

Letters are ideal for most matters. They are inexpensive (unlike lawsuits), they create a paper trail, and they have a good chance of landing on the right desk (unlike a phone call). Even letters that are not sent by lawyers can have a legal sting. Most people are surprised when I tell them that more than half the letters I write for my clients are not sent by me, but by the clients themselves. I suggest the words for such letters and sometimes even write the whole thing, but the clients send them on their own stationery. The recipients of these letters can usually tell that my clients have either spoken with a lawyer or are aware of the legal consequences of the matter. This will be the case with your letters. And because most people want to keep away from lawyers, most recipients of your letters will want to resolve the matter without further ado.

It *Is* the Money

I t makes the world go round. It talks. It changes everything. Keep it in mind because "it" is the most important thing in getting others to respond to your demands—*money*. The old saying "When someone says it's not about money, it's about money" is absolutely right. In nearly all situations involving business, money is the only consideration you face. What about reputation and goodwill? In my experience, these are important only when they affect money or power (which usually leads to money). When a lawyer is on the receiving end of a dispute (where I have been about half the time), clients don't pretend that things other than money—or things that generate money, such as jobs or election results—matter at all. You might like to think that people care about integrity and principles, but unfortunately, this is rarely the case.

Clients of mine who've received demands don't ask me, "Do you think she has a good point?" or "What do you think would be the fair thing to do here?" They ask, "What do you think is the cheapest way to get rid of this guy?" or "If we ignore them, will they have any sort of a case?" The bottom line is, I'm afraid, the bottom line.

Think Like a Lawyer

o lawyer worth his salt thinks only about what his client wants. If the world were designed to give my clients everything they want, they would not need me. A good lawyer always thinks about what the other party wants as well. Shopkeeper Joe may not give a hoot about my client as a human being, but he is smart enough to know that if he can make her happy he will save himself grief. Shopkeeper Joe, like everyone else, wants to save money and avoid trouble. Yes, there are some people who do the right thing just because it is right or because the law requires it or to protect their good names. But most are motivated by self-interest. My job is to show those people that they will suffer intolerable consequences (usually loss of money) if they don't meet my clients' demands. They usually see things my way: My clients get what they want; Shopkeeper Joe saves money and keeps his customers. Everybody wins. Often my work boils down simply to getting the attention of people who are too preoccupied to deal with small problems.

I prepare for each case I take on in the same way, whether it involves a multimillion-dollar lawsuit or a parking ticket. The steps I take will be the same ones you should take in your letter-writing campaigns. First, I shelve any strong emotions I might feel; they would only confuse my client's case. Then I determine what my client wants and what his opponent wants. I gather all the facts relating to the case and determine which ones are relevant. Then I analyze the facts and decide how best to present my case. Finally, I make my demand in the clearest possible terms and follow it up until I am satisfied with the results. All the while, I keep neat records of my contacts, leaving myself a useful paper trail.

Let's look at this process in closer detail and see how it relates to your letters.

Shelve your emotions. You may be enraged. You may be desperate, scared, and out of control. Your letters should not be. Histrionic letters do not get results. People who write in a rage usually do not have control of their thoughts. Their letters sound irrational and illogical. Effective letters are coherent, reasonable, and clear. Go to the gym, take a walk, or whine to your best friend about it, but get it out of your system before you sit down to write.

Determine what you want. The sweater you bought at Mom & Pop's Knit Shop had a big snag in it. Do you want

a new sweater? store credit? your money back? The airline
bumped you, causing you to miss an important meeting.
Do you want your money back? a free ticket to the same
location? a free ticket to another location? You can't get
what you want until you know what you want.

Determine what your opponent wants. What does
Mom & Pop's Knit Shop want: to keep you as a loyal customer? to avoid a trip to small claims court? Your HMO won't
cover the expense of a new medication you need. What does
your HMO want: to spend less money on the medication than
on litigation? not to be reported to a government watchdog
agency? Most opponents want to save money and
avoid hassles.

Review the facts. You went to Mom & Pop's Knit Shop
on Thursday after your trip to the gym. You tried on the sweater.
Angela waited on you. You paid with a credit card. What's
important here? Probably not that you had been at the gym.
Maybe not even that you tried on the sweater. Look at the
facts. Note important dates, times, names of people involved,
and other relevant details. Leave irrelevant details out of it.

Determine how to present your case. You've
known Mom and Pop for years. You shop at their store all the
time. A very simple, polite letter explaining your need to return

the sweater will probably do it. You've had trouble with your HMO for years and you know that it is under scrutiny by the regulatory agency. A strong, aggressive, take-no-prisoners letter detailing why the HMO must pay for your medication, with a photocopy to the regulators, is probably in order. (But as you will note in the sample letters, it is often best not to send a photocopy to a public agency the first time you write to the person you are complaining about. One of the things businesspeople like to avoid is having to deal with regulatory agencies, and this desire may work for you if you give the other person a chance to solve the problem himself.) Presenting your case is the crux of this book, so I will go into greater detail on how to do it effectively in the next section.

Be insistent and consistent. You've made your rational demands; you've kept a paper trail. Now it's time to follow up. You wait for a response and act accordingly. If in your letter you asked your HMO for a response within 72 hours, you must act when that time elapses. If Mom and Pop don't call right away, maybe you'll give them a week before following up. Follow up with polite but firm diligence until the matter is resolved.

The Effective Letter

The effective letter is the one that gets you what you want as quickly and easily as possible. Its format is perfect and its content persuasive. The following sections show exactly how to ensure that your letters are both. Before turning to the specific elements, note that there are several general points to remember.

Be concise. If a contract or lease or other document makes it clear that you are entitled to what you are trying to get, then the perfect letter simply states the facts, demands what you want, and accompanies a copy of the document with the relevant passages highlighted. This is not a case for experts or buzzwords or long explanations.

Be fair, reasonable, and appropriate. The way you present your letters (and thus yourself) is as important as the way you present the facts of your case. Your letters must be neat and professional. Your writing style must be clear. Your demands and the way you present them must reflect that you are a serious, intelligent, reasonable person. For example, a letter sent by certified mail, with return receipt requested, telling the owner of a carpet store that you have scheduled a conference at the Consumer Protection Division of the Attorney General's Office makes you appear irrational if your goal is simply to have him repair a few seams on the new job he installed for you. On the other hand, if you tell your HMO that you would very much appreciate hearing from it at its convenience regarding a matter that requires urgent care, you undermine yourself by appearing weak.

Make the tone and length of your letter appropriate to the problem. If your broken widget cost twenty dollars and Widgets-R-Us has a good reputation for returns, then a three-page tirade is probably overdoing it. On the other hand, a three-page tirade might be appropriate when addressed to an HMO that refuses to cover surgery that urgently needs to be performed.

The most effective letters are often the simplest.

You are not looking to win literary prizes for your letters. You don't need to show off to appear smart or worthy of a response. Use straightforward, polite prose. Forget the fancy words and long, complicated sentences. If you feel that colorful description adds to your case, then use it, as long as you are sure it doesn't cloud your point. (A client once described a tureen that a shipping company had broken as looking in worse shape than ancient pottery shards she had seen on a tour of Pompeii. It worked, but it would have been just as effective to say that the tureen had arrived in thousands of tiny pieces.) And please, don't try to write like a lawyer. Lawyers are notorious for being long-winded and overly complicated. Use our proven techniques, not our puffed-up prose.

Know your rights. Is your HMO required to cover name-brand prescription drugs? If it's not, your case in trying to make it do that is weakened. Has the warranty expired on the DVD player? If so, you'll have a hard time making a case that the manufacturer should fix it for free. You either have to demonstrate that you are in the right or base your case on something other than just the law.

Know your audience. Are you appealing to the proprietor of a small shop in your town or to the CEO of an international conglomerate? The way you make your case should be tailored to your audience.

A properly formatted letter shows seriousness, preparation for effective action, and good reasons to give you what you demand.

Format

Correct form does three things. First, it shows the recipient that you are serious. Sloppy or casual letters do not do this. Second, it lets the other person know that you are organized. It tacitly suggests that you are preparing evidence to take action if he does not respond favorably to you. Third, it helps clarify your points. It is the easiest part of your presentation, but it is also one of the most critical, because badly formatted letters are thrown away. Format alone cannot make your case, but it *can* break it.

Here are the rules of effective letter writing.

Type, don't write. If you don't have a computer or typewriter, borrow one or use the library's. Remember that the person who receives a letter from you can't tell whether you can type well or can only hunt and peck. As long as the letter comes out correctly, your typing skills don't matter. The important thing is that the finished product (letter and envelope) be free of mistakes.

Use a plain white 8½ x 11 sheet of paper. Serious letters arrive on serious paper. They do not arrive on undersize note cards or paper with pretty illustrations on it. Complaint letters usually go into boxes or files, so they are more likely to be lost if they are not the right size. If you have a business letterhead you prefer to use, that's fine, too.

Correct your grammar and spelling. Good grammar and perfect spelling are essential. If you have a track record as a poor speller, ask a friend or colleague to double-check your work. Proofread everything carefully for sense. Put yourself on the other side and ask what effect your letter would have on you if you were the recipient. If something sounds ridiculous to you when you reread it, change it or take it out. When you are satisfied that your letter will elicit the response you want, you are ready to mail it.

Indicate certified mail, return receipt requested. Often a letter that is written to demand that someone do something should be sent by certified mail, return receipt requested. This form of mailing does several things. It shows

Is Snail Mail the Only Way?

Like everyone else I know, I use e-mail all the time. But I don't recommend that you use e-mail for the type of letter this book is about. E-mail does not have the same sting as a letter, particularly one that arrives via certified mail. There is something about a postal carrier standing at the recipient's door, requiring that person to sign a receipt, that underscores the serious nature of your complaint. Since your letter has been written to get the recipient's attention and to spark action, e-mail is not deliberate enough. Although faxes are a little more convincing because they automatically produce hard copy, they still do not have the same effect as mailed letters. Faxes can be used when immediate delivery is necessary, as in disputes involving medical emergencies, but in those cases I prefer to use a private carrier (FedEx, UPS, and the like), which, like certified mail, requires a signature.

serious intent. People do not go to the post office, fill out papers, and pay a fee if they are not serious. In addition, this form of mailing provides proof that the addressee received your letter: The post office requires that someone sign when a letter sent in this fashion is delivered. When the return receipt comes back to you from the post office, staple it to your copy of the letter; it is proof that your letter was delivered on a particular date and that the person to whom you are writing knows this. Certified letters are heavy-handed, however. They may be too strong for a first attempt or if you are well acquainted with the person to whom you are writing. Note in the sample letters when certified mail is used and when it is not.

File under "Trash"

The chance that someone will respond to a letter is far greater when the letter is well formatted and properly addressed. Almost any businessperson you ask will admit to having thrown away letters that are sloppy or improperly addressed. The assumption is that if the writer is not capable of the simple task of presenting his case well, he will not have the stamina to follow through on his demands.

Address the right person or department. It is always best to write to a specific person, so if you can, get the name, title, and address of the person who ideally should handle your complaint. Don't be shy if it takes a phone call and a few transfers around the building to do so. If "Gerald C. Potter II,

A Properly Formatted Letter

Jane Doe
555 Main Street
Wherevertown, XX 55555
555-555-5555 tel
555-555-5550 fax

Certified Mail
Return Receipt Requested

January 5, 2003

Dr. Reader
Sample Corporation, Inc.
5 Business Road
Business City, XX 55555

Dear Dr. Reader:

This is a sample letter that reveals to you how to correctly format a letter. It is typed on a clean sheet of $8\frac{1}{2}$ x 11 paper with generous margins on all sides. The address of the writer is in the upper right-hand corner. There are two blank lines and then the certified mail designation appears on two lines flush left. After a one-line space, the date appears flush left. One blank below that is the name and address of the addressee. (Note that the writer has made the effort to find out that Dear Reader is a doctor.) One blank line follows the address, after which appears the salutation line. If you do not know specifically to whom you are writing, the line should say "Dear Sir or Madam." There is a line space and then the letter begins. The text is flush left and broken into paragraphs (in other words, new paragraphs are not indented; instead, there is a blank line between each paragraph). The signoff is "Sincerely," followed by the writer's signature (leave three to four lines blank for this) and then the typed name. If there are enclosures, that is noted below the signature, as are other recipients' names ("cc:").

Please format each letter you write this way. Make sure you check for spelling and grammar before you fold your letter into thirds and seal it in a business-size envelope, affix the postage, and mail it.

Thank you for your time and attention to this serious part of letter writing.

Sincerely,

Jane Doe

Enclosures

cc: John Q. Public

Vice President of Sales" receives a letter addressed in precisely that fashion, he is much more likely to respond than he is to one addressed to "Jerry Potter, Sales Department." If your claim is one you think will be somewhat routine, then an address of "Customer Service" and a salutation of "Dear Sir or Madam" is acceptable.

Use cc's. Many business letters end with something like "cc: Mr. Harry J. Smith, Department of Customer Relations" or "cc: Ms. Ethel P. Hallock, State Consumer Commission." These indications, which are known as "showing copies," mean that the person who is named after "cc:" (which means "carbon copy to") has been sent a copy of the letter. Usually that person was involved in the dispute or is in a position of authority to do something about it. The copies noted on the sample letters will give you a good idea of when it is appropriate to use them.

Making Your Case

T he law is about right and wrong. Right? Wrong. If there weren't so many gray areas, I'd be out of a job. The most enjoyable part of being a lawyer is making a case for my clients. In making a case, I interpret the law and the facts of the dispute in order to prove that my client is indeed right. When you write your letters, you are making a case for yourself.

In essence, a strong case consists of a demand, reasons, and evidence that are presented in a persuasive way. Here are all the things you need to do in order to present the strongest possible case for yourself in any dispute.

State your demand. Be clear about what you want. Explain that you are demanding an exchange, a refund, a response, a return of your deposit, to be released from the contract, et cetera. Make your demands absolutely clear, stick with them each time you write to the other person, and

---

Truth and Consequences

Most sales contracts don't allow consumers to get what are known as "consequential damages" because of a defective product. "Consequential damages" are money that someone loses because a defective product can't be used. For example, a carpenter who loses work because he can't use his newly purchased bench saw won't collect his lost profits in a court case. The best he can hope for is a repair or the refund of his purchase price.

---

don't compromise unless you are offered something that is really going to satisfy you. When there are several ways a person on the receiving end of a complaint can respond, he will give the best response to people who demand something specific. My clients offer the least to people who simply complain but don't indicate what they expect them to do. As George Bernard Shaw once noted, "Take care to get what you like, or you'll be forced to like what you get."

Just the Facts, Ma'am

The facts are the heart of your case. They should show that you are entitled to what you are asking and that you are serious, organized, and prepared to take action. Here are the important things to keep in mind as you present the facts:

1. Include all *relevant* details. Think like a journalist and report the whos, whats, wheres, and whens of your case. Include names, dates, and details. *Don't* include details that are irrelevant—in other words, those that are not clearly and directly related to the case.

2. Include copies of relevant paperwork. If there are receipts, letters, contracts, and so on, that support your case, include copies of them with your letter.

3. Tell what did not happen, as well as what did. A common example of this is when a complaint about something is made to an appropriate person and no response is received.

4. Check your logic. Ask yourself, "Do the facts I have reviewed say to any normal and reasonable person that someone who experienced what I have described has the right to what I'm seeking?" If so, you are good to go.

Document the facts. Your case should outline what happened or didn't happen to upset you. It should include as many names, dates, and details relating to the cause of your unhappiness as possible. If there is evidence in writing (contracts, receipts, and so on), you should make copies of these papers and include the copies. Do not include original merchandise or documents. Those are your evidence, and you may need them later.

Refer to the documents. The quickest way to end a dispute is to refer to a document that makes it clear that you are in the right. If you have such a piece of evidence, include a copy of it with your letter and make it the crux of your argument.

Document your opponent's refusal. A crucial part of documenting the facts is confirming in writing your opponent's refusal to meet your demand. Unless you live without a telephone, you have surely realized that the desire of businesses, public and private, is *not* to have to talk to you. In this climate it's not at all surprising that demands of dissatisfied customers and clients usually go unanswered. You must document all that your opponent refuses to do: take your calls, respond to letters, take action in regard to your complaint.

One of the requirements of nearly every legally valid claim (known as a "cause of action") is the refusal of the other person to meet your demand. If you take a look at lawsuits in courts, you will see this stated nearly every time. Lawsuits say, for example, that John did certain things that damaged Jane by a certain amount, and that after Jane approached him about it, *he refused to pay for the damages.* That the demand was not met says to the legal authorities that Jane is now entitled to seek official assistance.

You probably won't need to go to court, but the other person must always believe that you are prepared to do so and that, if you do, you will win. When the other person sees that you have confirmed his refusal to meet your demand (and especially if the other person's lawyer sees this), he will know how very serious you are.

Refer to the experts. One of the ways lawyers prevail is by relying on the opinions of experts. Sometimes experts are hired for the specific purpose of lending weight to a client's case. Sometimes an expert is simply someone who has knowledge of a client's situation and has an opinion that is favorable to the client's point of view.

Using experts to support your position isn't customary without involving a lawyer, but there is absolutely no reason not to do it to make a letter much stronger. For example, there is no reason why you could not hire a surveyor to help you in a dispute regarding a property line. There is no reason why you could not hire an appraiser to help you in a dispute involving the value of something. In these sorts of situations a carefully prepared letter from you that refers to the expert ("Albert Cummings, a carpenter with thirty years' experience, inspected your work and agrees that the job was not done properly") would be taken very seriously.

An Excerpt from a Letter That Won't Get Results

Mr. Robert Hawthorn
Sales Manager
Big Bob's Auto Agency
1000 Route 47 South
Detroit, Michigan 00000

Dear Mr. Hawthorn:

When my husband bought me a new Dinosaur automobile for my birthday in the same color as my sister's house, I never expected to have as much trouble as I have had with this car. This car has had all kinds of difficulties, including breakdowns, and has been in your shop at least five times in the past three months. I can't rely on it at all, and it's especially troublesome because I need to use it to visit my mother's house when she is sick. I wish my husband had never bought me this car and I would like you to fix it immediately or give me a new one.

Sincerely,

Roberta Scott

This letter is bad in several respects. First, the personal things about the car being a gift from her husband, the color of her sister's house, and her mother's sickness serve no purpose at all. Second, the letter is not specific about what went wrong with the car and the dates on which it was taken in for service. The sales manager will view this letter as coming from a lightweight and probably won't do much about it.

The person who receives such a letter also knows that there is no way he can continue stonewalling you unless he goes out and gets his own expert to support his position. At that point, in the hope of saving time and money, many of the people you deal with will agree to your demands.

In many cases an expert naturally becomes involved in your dispute. This is especially true in medical cases, where action cannot be delayed. Your HMO would have some trouble defending its refusal to send you to a dermatologist when the result of seeing one was that your rash was cured almost immediately. Any HMO with its wits about it would much rather pay your bill for the specialist and the medicine than deal with a medical malpractice claim.

Always, *always* get the expert's permission to use his name in your letters.

There is even the possibility of referring to an expert when the expert doesn't yet exist. This is most effective in a dispute in which you are clearly correct but the other person refuses to admit important facts. The trick is to offer a suggestion that any reasonable person would accept unless he knew it would not work in his favor. If the person you are trying to persuade refuses to accept your suggestion, you have proof of his unreasonableness. For instance, if the brick wall a builder made for you is badly constructed, suggest to the builder that the two of you select a master mason and ask him to examine the wall. Say that if the mason says the work was done well, you will pay the mason's inspection fee and drop your complaint; if not, the builder will pay the mason's fee and either correct the work or pay the master mason to do so.

Use your buzzwords. As I've said, you don't need to have a highfalutin writing style to make a clear case or to deserve attention. There is no substitute for simple, clear language. However, there are a few buzzwords that can act as a kind of shortcut to making your point. They are highly charged legal words and phrases that are sure to get attention. Buzzwords are particularly useful when you are writing to someone who deals with some form of state regulation or license requirement.

Take "wrongful denial," for example. These words strike fear in the hearts of insurance companies because an insurance company that wrongfully denies too many claims may lose its right to do business in your state. If you tell an insurance company that it owes you money for a claim, you may be whistling in a windstorm. But if you tell it that its failure to pay your claim is a "wrongful denial" of your claim, the person in the insurance company who reads your letter realizes that you know what you are talking about.

Buzzwords

Buzzword	Meaning	Context	Sample Sentence
wrongful denial	Not honoring a contract	When a claim is denied by an insurance company	*"Your company's refusal to compensate me for this loss is a wrongful denial of my claim."*
workmanlike fashion	Quality of work a contractor is expected to do	When a contractor fails to do satisfactory work	*"You didn't install the new furnace in our house in a workmanlike fashion."*
negligent	Performing responsibilities carelessly	When someone doesn't perform a job with sufficient care.	*"The work you did for us was performed in a negligent manner."*
grossly negligent	Performing responsibilities very carelessly	When someone doesn't perform a job with much care	*"The work you did for us was performed in a grossly negligent manner."*
recklessly indifferent	Performing responsibilities without any regard for proper performance	When someone doesn't perform a job with any care	*"The work you did for us was performed in a recklessly indifferent manner."*
standard of care	Accepted level of performance for doing something	When someone fails to do something with the amount of care generally expected in that sort of work	*"Your preparation of our tax returns didn't meet the standard of care for performing such work."*
lemon	An automobile that isn't satisfactory and can't be fixed by any repairs	When you purchase an automobile that is a lemon	*"The new car you sold me is a lemon and I demand the right to exchange it for another car."*
malpractice	Medical care that is not up to the required standard	When you receive poor medical care	*"I believe that your primary care physician is committing malpractice by failing to refer me to a specialist for the serious condition from which I am suffering."*
defective	A product that is not made correctly	When you purchase a product that does not do what it is supposed to do	*"The dishwasher I purchased from you is defective: It leaves soap powder on all of the dishes after it has washed them."*

BUZZWORDS

Buzzword	Meaning	Context	Sample Sentence
breach	A failure to honor a contract	When any part of your contract with someone has not been honored	*"The written one-year warranty you provided to us for this work has been breached since you are aware that the gutters leak and you have failed to repair them."*
hazardous	Dangerous to use or be around	When something someone has done leaves you with a dangerous situation	*"The electrical work you did at our house is hazardous because you left exposed wires in several places where we could touch them by mistake."*
improperly trained	Not competent to do a particular task	When a person without the proper training performs a particular task	*"It is obvious from the work that was done at our home that your electricians did not receive proper training."*
substantial performance	Reasonable completion of a job	When work has been accomplished to a reasonable extent even though there may be a few details left to be done	*"No one would consider that you have provided substantial performance of your contract to build an addition to our house."*
bad faith	Failure to try sincerely to meet the requirements of a contract	When someone's performance clearly shows that he did not care about the work	*"The number of mistakes you and your employees have made, and your repeated failure to correct them, indicates bad faith on your part."*
malicious	Done for a hurtful and improper purpose	When someone does something for the specific purpose of injuring you or so recklessly that he doesn't care if you're injured	*"Filing a lawsuit in this matter would simply be malicious and would serve no proper and useful purpose."*
groundless (or baseless)	Having no sensible and proper purpose	When someone does something that does not advance a valid legal objective	*"The claims that you are making against me are groundless and you know full well that there is no factual basis for them."*

Another example is "standard of care." Standard of care is the general expectation of state authorities that review HMO health care decisions and hear complaints against HMOs. If you write a letter to your HMO and advise it that your primary care physician didn't prescribe medicine for your aching muscles, you'd better hope that the over-the-counter products do the job for you. But if you say in your letter that your primary care physician did not comply with the "standard of care" for treating muscle pain like yours because she did not prescribe appropriate medication, your HMO may well tell your primary care physician to get out her prescription pad before your next visit. HMOs are aware that failure on the part of physicians to provide medical services that meet the standard of care may result in a claim for malpractice against them.

When a service is not rendered properly, the buzzwords "negligent," "grossly negligent," and "recklessly indifferent" can be useful. A person receiving a letter that uses such words knows how serious you are about what he failed to do, and he knows that you are aware that he did something wrong. In the case of a product you have purchased that does not do what it is supposed to do, the word "defective" is useful. The use of this word says to the person who reads your letter that you are aware of a flaw in the product and, very likely, of a breach in its guarantee or warranty. This is serious business for someone who makes things or sells them to members of the public. If the product is broken in a way that makes it dangerous, the use of the word "hazardous" is useful. This word suggests that you feel the product is dangerous for you or others. If you are correct about that, and if someone is hurt, the manufacturer or seller of the product who disregards your letter faces serious trouble.

Use buzzwords carefully; you will harm your case if you use them incorrectly. For instance, if a workman left a few trim pieces off of something he was installing for you, you would sound silly if you said that he was "recklessly indifferent" to his job. Accusing your doctor and HMO of "malpractice" because it was difficult for you to get an appointment at a convenient time only serves to make you look irrational. Remember, you want only the fulfillment of your reasonable expectations.

Keep good records. The more organized your record keeping, the more likely that you will be able to follow through effectively and win your case. If you do end up in court, your paper trail will be very persuasive.

In addition to keeping exact copies of each letter you write, together with the return receipts, and all documents that relate to what you are demanding

Stake Your Small Claims

In many states there is a small claims court, where nonlawyers can file lawsuits, handle their own cases, and receive money up to certain limits, such as $10,000 or $20,000. It isn't difficult to file these lawsuits, and many nonlawyers do so satisfactorily when all other efforts have failed. See appendix A for details on small claims courts.

(receipts, bills, relevant letters from you or others, et cetera), you should keep a log of your conversations. If you have a phone call that relates to the case, note the date, time, person's name, and what was said.

The Last Resort: When to Cry "Lawsuit"

Lawsuits are unpleasant, time-consuming, and expensive. My purpose in writing this book is to enable you to avoid them. However, sometimes when the stakes are high and when all else has failed, a lawsuit may be an option. Consider carefully these two caveats before you threaten your opponent with a lawsuit.

First, don't threaten a lawsuit if you are not entitled to file it. If you have any doubt about the matter, consult a lawyer before you make any form of threat. As a general rule, it is not lawful to file a lawsuit for any reason other than to obtain something to which you are legally entitled. You are *not* entitled to file lawsuits for the purpose of embarrassing or discrediting other people or to obtain things to which you are not legally entitled. A lawsuit that is threatened or filed for wrongful or malicious reasons can result in costs and penalties for the complainant.

Second, don't threaten a lawsuit unless you're prepared to file it. People who threaten lawsuits and have no intention of

What Not to Do

Don't threaten. There are so many reasons not to threaten. Here are a couple of persuasive ones: 1) You may be breaking the law in doing so, and 2) threatening letters may make you look like a nut, whereas polite letters may make people more likely to embrace your cause.

Don't insult. Never refer to anyone's race, religion, sex, or other personal characteristics. These things have absolutely nothing to do with your demand, and any reference to them will hurt your chances of getting what you want. Abusive people don't appear serious and rational. Furthermore, you don't know who will see the letter. Do you really want a regulator in a government agency to know you are a jerk?

Don't condescend. Condescension, sarcasm, and their like have no place in your letters. If you received a demand from a snide writer, would you want to help him or her? I can tell you from personal experience, letters written in an offensive tone go to the bottom of the "in" box if not the trash can.

pursuing them lose their leverage. Your opponent must believe that you are serious about everything you say, so a threat that turns out to be just hot air hurts your case.

There are three ways to threaten a lawsuit in a letter, and each of them is useful in the right circumstances. The first way to threaten a lawsuit is by not referring to a lawsuit at all but by saying that you hope that your demand will be met. ("I am writing this letter in the hope that an amicable resolution of this matter can take place.") The recipient gets the point. The second way to threaten a lawsuit is by saying something like the following: "If you do not properly repair our dishwasher by one week from today, we will be forced to take appropriate legal action." "Appropriate legal action" includes the possibility of a lawsuit, but it could mean other things as well. For example, you may live in a state where there is a consumer protection office that deals with complaints or a bonding requirement for contractors that do certain types of work. If there are several things you could do to push your demand, this sort of threat may raise concern by the other person about all the possibilities.

An advantage of the "appropriate legal action" threat is that it doesn't pin you down to a specific amount of money. It's often the case that your demand is not for money but for a specific action. You may demand of your HMO that it provide you with medical services. You may demand of your state public works department that it repair holes in the road in front of your house. If you threaten to take "appropriate legal action" if these things are not provided, the words you have used are satisfactory in light of the fact that you are not demanding a specific sum of money.

The third way to threaten a lawsuit is to do it outright in clear and unmistakable language. "If you don't forward the $2,371 to me immediately, I will file suit for this money and the costs to which I am entitled." This sort of statement certainly hits the other person between the eyes. It is appropriate when you have exhausted all other possibilities and you are prepared to close the door on further discussions and go to court. When the amount of money in question is what is known as a "liquidated" amount, which means an amount that is beyond any dispute, this way of threatening a lawsuit often makes sense. An advantage of this approach is that it makes it clear to the other person that the matter is going to court if you are not paid promptly. If there is absolutely nothing to argue about, this sort of threat very often results in the arrival of a check.

Another caveat regarding threats of lawsuits is important: There are situations in which a lawsuit may not be filed until certain things have happened. For example, HMO provider agreements often require you to use a certain review procedure before you are entitled to sue. Since this may be required by your contract, you should check the matter before threatening a lawsuit. In addition, many states have procedures for reviewing health care matters when they are disputed. Some of these procedures require certain things to occur before you have the right to file a lawsuit. These are things that vary from state to state, and you should check with the appropriate state office or a lawyer before threatening or filing this kind of lawsuit. There are lists of the responsible state agencies in appendix C.

Other Threats

You might be tempted to make threats other than those of lawsuits. My advice: Don't. You may be breaking the law.

One of my favorite threats is "I will have your license revoked!" A private citizen can't speak for what a public official will do. You are the owner of your own private rights, and you may enforce them by an appropriate lawsuit. You don't control the insurance commission, the taxation authority, the health regulatory agencies, the contractor licensing office, or any other public agency. When a private citizen threatens to involve a public agency, or even simply to inform a public agency, that person is threatening something he or she has no power to control.

That said, there are two important things you should know that will make you feel better about this matter.

First, you are entitled to give accurate information concerning another person to the responsible public agency and seek that agency's help and guidance to the extent

Not for Your Eyes Only

In ordinary correspondence, only two people come into the picture: the person who sends the letter and the person who receives it. That is not always the case with complaint letters.

If you write to an employee of a large corporation, it is likely that to deal with your demand, several other people will have to see your letter. (If you write a letter to the self-employed plumber who botched your sink repair, the odds are he'll be the only person ever to see it.) If your letter makes it clear that legal action is possible, a lawyer will almost certainly review it, too.

it is available. For example, almost every state has available in one of its agencies (sometimes the Office of the Attorney General) an office that is responsible for consumer protection matters. If you have been misled about something you purchased or if you have purchased something that is defective,

---

An Excerpt from an Inappropriate and Ineffective Letter

Mr. Matthew Hyde
Ace Plumbing Company
765 York Road
Wildwood, New Jersey 00000

Dear Mr. Hyde:

I have asked your company on three occasions to fix the leaks in the new bathroom where you installed the plumbing fixtures. Each time your service people come to our house they look completely disgusting and I don't even want to let them in. One of the men who works for you does not act right and another man has a very bad smell. Each time they leave the house the leaks continue and my wife and I are getting fed up. If you don't do something immediately to fix this problem, I will have to do something about you and your disgusting crew.

Sincerely,

Carl Warner

This letter makes an unnecessary and personal attack on the work people. Comments like this only serve to make the writer look bad and the addressee defensive. Also, the writer does not state what the specific problems are and he is vague about what he wants done. This writer has not done his homework, and he will not get the results he seeks.

and the seller will not fix it or take it back, you have the right to advise your state's consumer protection office and ask for its assistance. When you ask for such assistance, do so respectfully and follow the instructions the public agency gives you.

Second, you should be aware that there are state agencies devoted to handling certain kinds of disputes. Many states have consumer protection offices. Every state has one or more agencies that deal with health care providers. In some states there are offices for the specific purpose of resolving health care coverage disputes with health care providers. All states have agencies that deal with big businesses such as banks, insurance companies, and public utilities. State real estate commission offices are available to handle problems that occur with regard to house contracts and deposit disputes. Many of these are listed in appendix C. If you don't find what you need there, a telephone call to your state representative's office or an information service in your state government should be sufficient to advise you if there is an office that deals with the matter that concerns you.

You may want to alert your opponent that you have contacted the appropriate agency. Do not threaten him. Do not refer to the possible consequences he may suffer. Simply report factual information. ("I have contacted the Liquor Control Board and have been advised that . . .") License holders don't want to risk losing their licenses. Businesses that need state approval to continue operating can't risk losing that approval. You don't need to tell such people these things, and you are taking needless chances if you do.

At this point, the other person will almost always meet your demand. The only thing that remains for you to do when that happens is be sure that you have correctly ended the matter with the public agency. So that you can never be accused of using the public agency improperly, be sure to tell your contact there when your demand has been met and ask him to advise you about the proper way to close the matter. Follow the public agency's advice exactly, and let the other person know that you have done so.

Case Closed: The Settlement Letter

The letters you send will elicit responses. In most cases your demands will be met. In others you may be willing to compromise.

Whether you end a dispute by getting everything you want or by compromising, it is important that you confirm your agreement promptly and in writing. I am calling this a "settlement" even though in many situations you will receive everything you demand. It is important to send written confirmation of the settlement because people are busy and have short memories, especially when they have to get out their checkbooks. Also, it is possible that other people will enter the picture and not be familiar with what has been agreed. People change jobs; companies are restructured or taken over. You want to make sure your agreement is upheld under any conditions that may arise.

A settlement letter should refer to the precise conversation or letter from the other person that settled the matter. It should indicate that you have accepted the settlement provided it is carried out promptly. If there is any doubt, you'd better define what "promptly" means, since people often disagree about this. If you want to be formal about the matter and have doubts regarding the other person's intention to keep the settlement agreement, ask the other person to sign a copy of your letter and return it to you. If a third party needs to know about the settlement agreement in order for it to work out, be sure to send that person a copy of your letter.

The Letters

Now we come to the meat of the matter. The letters that follow are closely based on those that I have written for my clients, and they have gotten results every time. Obviously, you will have different disputes with your HMO, with people who sell you things that are defective, and with people who do poor work. You will have different problems with banks, insurance companies, and other businesses. The sample letters will show you how to apply my methods to your own situations. Each of the letters features comments that discuss why it is effective and how to tailor it for different needs.

The letters are organized by type of situation. Within each situation there are different letters for different sorts of circumstances. There is a letter for most of the types of situations you will face. When your situation is different from any letter, there should be a letter that is close enough that it should work with a few modifications.

Use these sample letters the same way lawyers use forms, crossing out the words that don't apply to your particular situation and replacing them with words that do apply. Or if you prefer, you can use them as loose guidelines and be freer with your language. Obviously dates, names, and addresses must be replaced with the correct ones.

1. Letter to retailer who sold defective items:

July 12, 2003

Mr. Arthur C. Scott
Manager ❶
The Wooly Mammoth
9283 James Street
Burlington, Vermont 00000

Dear Mr. Scott:

ANALYSIS

❶ This letter is addressed to the manager of the store where you purchased the sweaters. A letter to a particular person is always more effective. You can learn the names of people such as store managers simply by making a phone call.

On July 8, 2003, I purchased two cashmere sweaters in your store. Two days later, I wore one of the sweaters for the first time and noticed when I took it off that the dye appeared to be fading on some parts of the sweater. When I examined the other sweater, I noticed the same thing.

I telephoned your store the next day and described the salesperson who had sold me the sweaters. I was told that he no longer works for you and my call was transferred to Mr. Jerome Closs. Mr. Closs told me that the sweaters were of extremely high quality and that the dye in them would not fade under any circumstances. He said that the sale was final because it was a clearance sale, so there was no point in my bringing the sweaters in for him to evaluate.

I have been a loyal customer of your store for many years and have never had anything but good experiences with your sales staff. I hope that in light of this good relationship you will call or write to me to arrange a time when I may come in to present the defective sweaters for your inspection and receive a full refund. ②

I enclose copies of my bill of sale and credit card receipt with this letter and look forward to hearing from you at your earliest convenience.

Sincerely,

Ann C. Barker

Enclosures ③

2. Letter to retailer who sold defective items and did not respond to first letter:

August 1, 2003

<u>Certified Mail</u> ❶
<u>Return Receipt Requested</u>

Mr. Arthur C. Scott
Manager
The Wooly Mammoth
9283 James Street
Burlington, Vermont 00000

Dear Mr. Scott:

On July 12, I sent you a letter regarding two defective sweaters I purchased at your store. It has been more than two weeks and I have not heard from you. ❷

ANALYSIS

❶ This letter is sent by certified mail, return receipt requested; Ms. Barker is now getting serious because her first letter received no response. A certified letter advising someone that the consumer protection division of the attorney general's office has become involved will almost always get that person's attention.

ANALYSIS

❷ This is a follow-up letter. It refers specifically to Ms. Barker's earlier letter by date.

I have contacted the Consumer Protection Division of the Attorney General's Office and asked for advice. Mr. Charles H. Wormly advises that we proceed with a hearing to resolve the matter, so you will receive a letter from him very soon to schedule a date. **3** He has asked me to call him to cancel the meeting if you and I reach a resolution before that time. **4**

I hope we can resolve this without his intervention so we can both avoid the hassle and expense a hearing will surely bring.

Sincerely,

Ann C. Barker

cc: Mr. Charles H. Wormly **5**

ANALYSIS

3 This letter does not make a threat to Mr. Scott, but simply advises him what Ms. Barker has done and what Mr. Wormly of the Consumer Protection Division told her.

ANALYSIS

4 It is important to state in letters like this that the person in the public office advised you that the hearing would be canceled if the matter is resolved. The person who receives a letter like this now has to take into account the time and expense the hearing will involve and also the likelihood that he will be told to take the sweaters back.

ANALYSIS

5 The use of "cc: Mr. Charles H. Wormly" lets Mr. Scott know that you are keeping Mr. Wormly advised.

ANALYSIS

Note that if Ms. Barker had sent the sweaters with her first letter, she would have no evidence at a hearing.

3. Letter to mail-order company that misled purchaser about item ordered:

Mr. Price knows he is on shaky ground because of the 30-day limitation on refunds, which he did not observe. Even though he has a good reason for delay in returning the shelving kit, it is always better to obey the terms of sale that are stated in writing. Mr. Price has taken his best shot by doing several things in his letter.

July 27, 2003

Customer Service Department
Out of the Closet
2525 Merritt Boulevard
Boston, Massachusetts 00000

Dear Sir or Madam:

I receive your mail-order catalog regularly and have enjoyed ordering items from it in the past. That changed three days ago.

On May 21, I received a catalog number 438279F from you. That day I ordered from it a shelving kit that the catalog said was suitable for use in any closet. The picture in the catalog showed the fully assembled shelves, which did not reveal any wall fasteners. ① I paid for the kit with my Visa card. ②

Your description and picture of the shelving unit misled me into believing that the shelves support themselves. When I went to assemble the shelves, I learned that brackets needed to be screwed to the inside of the closet for the shelves to be used. I ordered these shelves because they did not seem to require screws. Because one wall of my closet is made of brick, it is nearly impossible to screw anything into it.

On July 24, 2003, I telephoned your 800 number and requested instructions as to how to return this item. I was told by the person answering the telephone that I would not be permitted to return the item since I had kept it for over 30 days. Thirty days? I didn't receive the shelves for about ten days, immediately after which time I went on vacation (it is the summer,

ANALYSIS

① He has explained why the catalog was misleading to him. Even though it would be an uphill fight for Mr. Price to prove what lawyers call fraud, the catalog company might give Mr. Price a refund in order to avoid the argument.

ANALYSIS

② Mr. Price has noted that he paid for the shelving kit with his Visa card. Credit card companies have various arrangements for dealing with unsatisfactory purchases by cardholders. The catalog company is aware of this and may not want to waste the time getting into the matter with Visa even though the company may win in the end.

after all). I returned from my vacation to juggle not only my busy schedule, but also the large, complicated shelving unit (which was, as I described to you, unlike what was pictured in the catalog), trying to make it work for my closet before giving up. Under the circumstances, thirty days hardly seems like a fair length of time—especially for a loyal customer.

If I have to take this up with Visa, I will. If I have to take it up with a lawyer, I will. It would be easiest, of course, for you to be reasonable and accept the return of merchandise that was purchased in good faith by a good customer.

Please let me know by August 12 whether or not we'll be able to handle this between ourselves.

Sincerely,

Matthew Price

4. Letter to dealer that sold defective refrigerator:

February 19, 2002

Mr. Jack M. Crawford
Manager
Austin Appliances, Inc.
24 Dorsey Road
Washington, DC 00000

Dear Mr. Crawford:

As you know, I purchased an expensive refrigerator from you on January 17, 2002. I am enclosing copies of the invoice and credit card receipt for the refrigerator.

The refrigerator hasn't worked properly since you delivered it on January 22. I have called your service department three times to tell you that the refrigerator won't keep a constant temperature. On February 4 and February 11 your repairmen came to our house and tried to fix it and left thinking they had. They hadn't. Your efforts have done no good. The refrigerator still won't keep a constant temperature, and the food in it has been ruined several times.

I have looked through the materials you gave me when I purchased the refrigerator. In those materials is a manufacturer's warranty that says "all mechanical components of this product are guaranteed against defects in design and workmanship for a period of one year." It is pretty obvious that the guarantee is not being honored, since this refrigerator is defective, unfixable, and has not been replaced. **1**

I have already lost quite a bit of food because of the problem, and I obviously need a properly working refrigerator to keep food in the house. **2** I expect this refrigerator to be replaced no later than next Monday. If this does not occur, I will be forced to discuss the matter with my lawyer **3** and take whatever legal action she indicates is appropriate. I look forward to hearing from you by March 1, 2002, as to how you would like to handle this matter.

Sincerely,

Wilma L. Brenner

Enclosures **4**

ANALYSIS

1 By quoting from the manufacturer's warranty, Ms. Brenner is letting the dealer know that she is a serious person and has taken time to understand her legal rights.

ANALYSIS

2 By referring to the spoiled groceries, Ms. Brenner is letting the dealer know that she has suffered financial harm as a result of this defective product.

ANALYSIS

3 Ms. Brenner refers to "my lawyer." Even if you don't have a lawyer and would have to go out and find one, suggest that you do. It sounds much stronger to indicate that you already have a relationship with an attorney.

ANALYSIS

4 By enclosing copies of the invoice and credit card receipt, Ms. Brenner is showing the dealer that she is ready for action. It is unlikely that any dealer would ignore a letter like this since he would know that Ms. Brenner's threat to use a lawyer and take legal action is a real threat

5. Letter to national company complaining of lack of response of local dealer:

March 23, 2003

<u>Certified Mail</u>
<u>Return Receipt Requested</u>

Mr. Jack A. Abbott
Customer Relations Manager
ABC Sales, Inc.
2400 Market Street
Reston, Virginia 00000

Dear Mr. Abbott:

I am writing to you because I am unable to solve a problem my wife and I are having with your local dealer on Branchwood Road here in Boston. **1** I will describe the difficulties we are having and tell you what we demand be done about it.

ANALYSIS

1 This letter is deliberately written to go above the head of the local dealer. When you have difficulties with someone in a part of a national business, this approach may be very useful. The local dealer is probably thinking about his own profits, but the national dealer usually thinks about the reputation of the entire company.

On September 17, 2002, my wife and I selected fabric
at your dealer for curtains for our bedroom and master bedroom. We agreed that a representative from
your dealer would come to our house to measure the
windows and would install the curtains once they
were made. The price we agreed on included all of
the fabric, making the curtains, and installing the
curtains. I am enclosing a copy of the invoice we
received when this order was placed.

On November 6, 2002, Mr. Snowden of your dealer
telephoned us to say that the fabric had arrived. He
told us at that time that the fabric was slightly different in color from the one we selected because the dye
lot was different. He asked if one of us could stop by
the store before the curtains were made to be sure
that the new fabric was acceptable to us. My wife did
that two days later, and Mr. Snowden showed her a
sample of the fabric that had arrived. The sample was
very close to the color we selected, and my wife said
to go ahead and make the curtains.

On February 12, 2003, Mr. Snowden telephoned us
and said that the curtains were finished and ready to
be installed. We agreed that someone from the dealership would come here on February 24, 2003, to install
the curtains in both rooms.

On February 24, 2003, two installers arrived and
installed the curtains. I was at work at the time, and

my wife had to leave the house for a doctor's appointment about 20 minutes after the two men arrived. No one was in the house for the rest of the time except our daughter.

When my wife and I saw the curtains that evening, we realized that they were not what we had ordered— nor were they something anyone would have ordered: Part of the fabric was the same color we had originally selected and part of it was the new color.

My wife telephoned Mr. Snowden on February 25, 2003, and told him that the curtains were unacceptable because of the two different colors of fabric. Mr. Snowden said that no one in your dealership thought the variation in color was extreme, and since this was a custom job he would not remove the curtains and give us a credit. I telephoned Mr. Snowden later that day and told him that we did not agree with him about the matter and we intended to pursue it. I told Mr. Snowden that there was no way we would accept the curtains in their current condition.

We have done two things since our conversations with Mr. Snowden. We asked a reputable curtain manufacturer to look at the curtains and tell us whether he feels they are acceptable. This man visited our home and looked at the curtains and immediately said he would not accept them if he were in our position. ② In addition, we contacted our lawyer about this matter and told her that we may be seeking her help. She told us that we should make one more try to resolve the matter by writing to you and explaining our dissatisfaction with your dealer. We have taken our lawyer's advice and we hope that you will review this matter very carefully in the next week and let us know if legal action will be necessary.

Sincerely,

George C. Marshall

cc: Draperies, Etc., Inc. ③
Attention: Mr. Franklin Snowden

ANALYSIS

② The use of someone else in the curtain business is important in a letter like this because there are differences of opinion in matters like how much change in color causes something to be unsatisfactory. A customer's opinion about such a matter may be suspect, whereas the opinion of a dealer is usually more convincing.

ANALYSIS

③ When you write a letter like this, you should be sure to copy the local dealer as Mr. Marshall has done. This lets the local dealer know that it now has problems with its national office as well as with you. The national office may tell the local dealer that it does not want to get into a legal fight with Mr. Marshall, especially a fight where another dealer is going to say that the work was not satisfactory.

6. Letter to car manufacturer regarding defective car not fixed or replaced by dealer:

January 4, 2003

Certified Mail ❶
Return Receipt Requested

Mr. Eugene H. Struthers ❷
Customer Relations Manager
Pioneer Auto Manufacturing
    Company
17500 Deer Park Road
Detroit, Michigan 00000

Dear Mr. Struthers:

I purchased a 2002 Blowfish automobile at Blank Motors of 555 Sunset Strip, Plymouth, New York, on September 12, 2002. The automobile has serial number 298763415293-HRQ. It has not operated properly since I purchased it.

On September 22, 2002, the exhaust system came loose from the engine when the car went over a small bump. The dealer looked at it and found it had not been attached correctly.

On October 3, 2002, the left rear brake began leaking brake fluid, so the dealer had to replace the brake cylinder and do work on the brake lining.

On October 18, 2002, the car stopped running altogether. I had to have it towed to the dealer, who found that the computer that sets the engine timing was not working properly. The computer was replaced.

On November 8, 2002, the car overheated five minutes after it was started. The dealer found that the hoses in the cooling system were not correctly connected.

In December 2002, the transmission began slipping and finally stopped shifting gears in the normal fashion. The dealer adjusted the transmission on two occasions that month but it is still not working.

The dealer advised me that it will not replace this car with a new one, since it has repaired each problem as it has occurred. I am not satisfied with that. The total number of items that have broken in this car is shameful, and the transmission is still not working properly. The car is obviously a lemon, ③ and I don't have the time or patience to spend the rest of my life having it towed to the dealer and waiting for repairs to be made.

I cannot tell you how disappointed I am in what has happened with this car. I selected it from many competitive models that I seriously considered. Your dealer has a good reputation, and I would assume that this is the sort of matter it would resolve very promptly. ④

Please review this matter promptly and advise me in writing if you will arrange to have this car replaced with a new car at no expense to me. If this doesn't happen, I am going to consult a lawyer and take appropriate steps to enforce my legal rights.

Sincerely,

Josephine B. Black

cc: Blank Motors ⑤

ANALYSIS

③ The word "lemon" is a useful buzzword in letters like this, since there are laws that require automobile manufacturers to exchange cars under certain circumstances when they are deemed faulty. The long history of difficulties in the first few months after this car was purchased is important to show that it is a lemon.

ANALYSIS

④ The next-to-last paragraph in this letter is emotional, but it does not detract from the legal force of the letter. Some people will be affected by such statements and others will not.

ANALYSIS

⑤ Be certain to send a copy to the car dealer and use the "cc:" notation to show the automobile manufacturer that you did so.

7. Letter to television manufacturer regarding warranty claim:

Whenever you make a claim for breach of a warranty, be certain that you read the warranty carefully and make your claim in light of it. In a situation like this, where the time it took to receive the television extended the time period beyond the 90 days for complete warranty, the argument made here is reasonable, and Mr. Nelson sets it forth properly. Although the warranty may use words like "90 days from the date of purchase" and "the time of repair," reasonable people could interpret the 90-day full-service warranty as running from the time Mr. Nelson received the television until the time it broke.

October 19, 2003

Certified Mail **1**
Return Receipt Requested

Mr. Maxwell Holmes
Customer Service Manager
Vivid Television
    Manufacturing, Inc.
1000 Defense Highway
Lansing, Michigan 00000

ANALYSIS

1 Both federal and state authorities can conceivably come into play with regard to a manufacturer's warranty that is not honored (or is interpreted to destroy its value and effectiveness). Mr. Nelson's letter (sent by certified mail, return receipt requested) alerts the manufacturer to the possibility of difficulties. Manufacturers often prefer to resolve a single problem rather than face the possibility that a regulatory agency will review their conduct generally. Mr. Nelson has chosen not to cc a regulatory agency in his first letter, in the hope that the manufacturer will act quickly to ensure that no one else becomes involved in the dispute.

Dear Mr. Holmes:

I purchased a wide-screen television made by your company on July 4, 2003. The television was delivered to my house on July 10, 2003. The warranty that came with the television says that it is completely guaranteed for 90 days and thereafter contains a parts guarantee for the balance of one year. The television stopped working 88 days after I received it, and I telephoned your service department the next day. I am now being told that since I did not call you before 90 days expired after the date of sale—not delivery—the only guarantee I have is the parts guarantee. I was told that the service required to fix this television will cost $382, and the broken part, which is apparently a minor part, will be free.

A 90-day full guarantee must mean 90 days from the date I received my television. If the dealer is unable to deliver it for six days, that is certainly not my fault. You are interpreting the warranty on this television in a way that makes it useless. I appreciate your providing the minor part at no charge, but that is not at all reasonable in light of the price of this television ($2,275) and the warranty that came with it.

I want to resolve this matter with you amicably if possible. If you want to do this, please telephone

Mr. Emile Snodgrass at your local repair facility and advise him that my television is to be repaired at no charge. If you choose not to do this, I can assure you that I will pursue other avenues until I receive what I am entitled to under my warranty. I certainly hope that will not be necessary.

Sincerely,

Stuart C. Nelson

8. Letter demanding right to return used car:

September 14, 2002

<u>Certified Mail</u>
<u>Return Receipt Requested</u>

Mr. Gerald Schaeffer
Schaeffer Used Cars
9459 Bishop Highway
Detroit, Michigan 00000

Dear Mr. Schaeffer:

Two weeks ago I purchased a used Moonbeam car from you for $2,750. You told me that you had inspected the car and it was in running condition. The odometer in the car said it had 53,000 miles on it.

Two days after I got the car home the crankshaft went bad. The whole engine needs to be rebuilt or replaced, and this will cost at least $1,500.

When the car broke down it was towed to Hobbs Auto Repair on the highway. You probably know that Mr. Hobbs has about as much experience with used cars as anybody you'll ever meet. Mr. Hobbs told me that if this car has less than 100,000 miles on it, then he is Napoleon. He said that the engine in this car looked about as bad as any engine he has seen in many years. I am sure you didn't realize this when you sold me the car.

I don't want to go through all the expense and hassle of litigation if it can be avoided. If you return the money I paid to you and take the car back, it will end the matter. If you agree that handling this matter the easy way is the best course of action, please call me as soon as possible after you receive this letter.

Sincerely,

Arnold H. Pointer

2

9. Letter to parking lot company that damaged car:

November 1, 2003

<u>Certified Mail</u>
<u>Return Receipt Requested</u>

Mr. Joseph Blackburn
Metropolitan Parking Lots, Ltd.
210 Water Street
Washington, DC 00000

Dear Mr. Blackburn:

I understand that you are the owner of the parking lot on the west side of Smith Avenue directly adjoining Howard Street. I am writing to demand compensation for the damage that was done to my car when I parked there last Saturday evening to go to a movie theater.

As my wife and I returned from the movie at about 11:00 P.M., your parking lot attendant was moving an automobile from the opposite side of the aisle in order to get another customer's car out of its space. In doing this, he put the car he was moving in reverse and pressed down so hard on the accelerator that a very loud screech came from the tires spinning on the pavement, and a six- or eight-foot-long rubber mark was left on the pavement. I saw your attendant smash my car in the hood and right front fender area. When I walked into the lot and spoke to your attendant, he did not deny hitting my car but said, "I don't think I hit it very hard." In fact, he knew full well that he had hit it hard, and the damage to my car was obvious.

Anyone seeing, as I did, the manner in which your attendant backed the car out of the space and struck mine would conclude that he was reckless and grossly negligent. ❶ Had anyone been behind the car he was driving, she might well have been killed. Not only did my wife and I witness your attendant's driving, but a man named Irving Sutterly, who was kind enough to give us his name and address, saw it as well. ❷

ANALYSIS

❶ Ticket stubs in parking lots, like many documents you receive these days, contain what is known as an "exculpatory clause." An exculpatory clause says that no matter how much damage you are caused by something such as an injury to your car in a parking lot, you can only recover a limited amount or nothing. The law in most states upholds these clauses, unfair though they are. The best hope of getting around them is to allege recklessness or gross negligence, which sometimes are not covered by the exculpatory clause.

ANALYSIS

❷ Mr. Willis has acted wisely by giving the name of a third party, as well as himself and his wife, who saw the incident. Mr. Blackburn will know that he is serious about the matter and is prepared for further action.

I am enclosing an estimate for repairs to my car, which you will note comes to $1,892.50. **3** I expect to receive a check from you for this amount promptly. If that does not occur, I will pursue appropriate legal action. **4**

Sincerely,

Harry A. Willis

Enclosure

ANALYSIS

3 In any instance like this, always document the precise damages carefully by getting an estimate or other appropriate writing.

ANALYSIS

4 Every form of business, including parking lots, is regulated by some state or city agency. The conduct of Mr. Blackburn's attendant certainly would not do him any good if it came to the attention of the proper agency. Mr. Blackburn knows that "appropriate legal action" could involve informing the agency of what occurred.

10. Letter to plumber who did faulty work:

October 10, 2003

<u>Federal Express</u>

Mr. Jason Hardridge
Hardridge Plumbing
2916 St. Monica Drive
New Freedom, Pennsylvania 00000

Dear Mr. Hardridge:

On September 12, 2003, my wife and I hired you to install new plumbing fixtures in our downstairs bathroom. The fixtures consisted of a sink, toilet, and small shower unit. We purchased the fixtures separately at Home Depot, and you installed them on September 14 and 15, 2003, ❶ for an agreed fee of $925, plus $102.46 for miscellaneous parts.

	ANALYSIS
❶	By being precise about dates, Mr. Smith is letting Mr. Hardridge know that he is keeping a careful record.

We paid your bill for this work on September 16, 2003 (check number 4321).

On October 5, 2003, less than a month after you completed this work, difficulties came to our attention with regard to both the toilet and the shower. The toilet drain was not installed correctly, and the toilet backs up and overflows. The hot-water faucet of the shower leaks. The leak appears to be coming from where the faucet was connected to the pipe inside the wall. The work on these two items was clearly defective. ❷

On October 6, 2003, my wife phoned your office and left a message on your voice mail telling you about these problems. She requested that you schedule a time to repair the work.

On October 8, 2003, I made a second call to your office and spoke with your wife. I told her that you had not yet responded to my wife's telephone call and that we needed you to come immediately.

We have had no answer to these telephone calls, and the work remains defective and causing serious problems.

If I do not hear from you within the next 48 hours, ❸ I will be forced to hire another plumber to fix these problems. **4** If that occurs, I will bill you for the full expense.

I feel terrible that our relationship has come to this point, since you were so highly recommended to me by several people. I sincerely hope we will be able to resolve the matter without further difficulty. **5**

Sincerely,

John R. Smith

ANALYSIS

4 Mr. Smith's statement that he may have to hire another plumber is useful because Mr. Hardridge knows very well that the new plumber will be a witness to the defective work.

ANALYSIS

5 It never hurts to mention that someone was favorably recommended to you and that you feel particularly bad because of that. Don't threaten to tell the person who recommended the plumber or anyone else about what has occurred. The plumber will worry about his reputation and recommendations in any event, whereas you don't want to be accused of disparaging someone.

11. Letter to plumber who did not answer first letter:

A follow-up letter in situations like this is rarely necessary. Most contractors will repair defective work before another contractor gets to do it. When that does not happen, a letter like this, demanding that you be paid for the repair cost, is necessary.

October 15, 2003

Certified Mail
Return Receipt Requested

Mr. Jason Hardridge
Hardridge Plumbing
2916 St. Monica Drive
New Freedom, Pennsylvania 00000

Dear Mr. Hardridge:

I am writing to let you know that my wife and I hired another plumber on October 14, 2003, to repair the broken toilet and shower that you installed. That plumber has advised us that your work was improper in several respects. The toilet was not seated properly when you installed it, and the drain was not connected correctly. You also failed to properly fasten the hot-water faucet in the shower to the hot-water pipe, and the result was a permanent leak at the joint. The repair of both items cost $563.87. I enclose a bill. ❶

I am very disappointed not only in your poor work but in your handling of the matter. Neither the two phone calls my wife and I placed to you nor the letter I sent on October 10 were answered. If the enclosed bill is not paid within five days, we will pursue appropriate legal action. ❷

Sincerely,

John R. Smith

ANALYSIS

❶ You have the economics of the matter as an ally when you write such a letter. It would be less expensive for Mr. Hardridge to pay you the $563.87 than it would be to hire a lawyer and spend time defending the case.

ANALYSIS

❷ The use of the words "appropriate legal action" let Mr. Hardridge know that his contractor's bond may be at risk if he does not send you the check. If it is not necessary to make a specific threat in order to accomplish your purpose, you should not consider making it.

12. Letter to HVAC contractor who installed defective product:

This letter does not threaten anything. It advises Mr. Nelson that you have gotten a state office involved in the problem. It also advises Mr. Nelson that he can avoid the hearing if he properly repairs the new furnace. Since Mr. Nelson knows very well that his chances of succeeding at the hearing are very small, and that his license to do HVAC work might somehow be in jeopardy if he was found to be incompetent, the odds are very high that Mr. Nelson will fix the furnace before the date of the hearing.

January 24, 2003

Certified Mail
Return Receipt Requested

Mr. Charles H. Nelson
Custom HVAC, Inc.
313 Townsend Avenue
Madison, Wisconsin 00000

Dear Mr. Nelson:

My husband and I have run out of patience trying to solve the problem we have been having with you. The new furnace you installed at our home hasn't worked from the moment it was installed on November 5, 2002. We have discussed this matter with you countless times and have also written to you about it. The furnace still doesn't operate correctly, and our house is bitterly cold most of the time.

I have brought this matter to the attention of the Consumer Protection Division of the State Attorney General's Office. Mr. Harold Blanchard of that office will be scheduling a hearing in this matter, most likely during the week of March 7. If the new furnace is satisfactorily repaired before the date of the hearing, I will alert Mr. Blanchard that a hearing isn't necessary.

I am sorry that our difficulties have come to this point, but you have really left us with no choice.

Sincerely,

Natalie R. Williams

cc: Mr. Harold Blanchard ❶

13. Letter to trucking company that damaged furniture:

March 23, 2003

Certified Mail
Return Receipt Requested

Mr. Robert Culpepper
Manager
Jones Trucking Company
2916 Esther Place
Lexington, Kentucky 00000

Dear Mr. Culpepper:

Our furniture was shipped by your company from Binghamton, New York, to El Paso, Texas. The furniture was picked up in Binghamton on March 12, 2003, and delivered to us in El Paso on March 18, 2003. When the furniture arrived two of our dining room chairs were badly damaged and our love seat had a wet stain on the left-hand cushion that cannot be removed. I provided this information to your local representative in El Paso on March 20, 2003, by telephone.

The two dining room chairs are beyond repair. I asked a local furniture store to let me know the cost of replacing them. I enclose a copy of its estimate.

The love seat is a good one and we can continue to use it, but it must be reupholstered. A business that does that here in El Paso has given me a proposal with similar-quality fabric. I am also enclosing a copy of that information.

As you can see, the cost of replacing the two dining room chairs that were broken by your company and reupholstering the love seat that was permanently stained comes to $971.43. This is the amount you owe us for the damage that was done to our furniture. If you want to inspect these items, they are in our garage here in El Paso and we will keep them there for the next ten days to give you or your insurance company the opportunity to do that. ❷

Sincerely,

Marilyn Rodgers

Enclosures ❸

14. Letter to garden service that performed carelessly:

November 7, 2002

<u>Certified Mail</u>
<u>Return Receipt Requested</u>

Ms. Jessica Johnson
Johnson Landscaping Company
123 Beaver Dam Road
Cleveland, Ohio 00000

Dear Ms. Johnson:

I have spoken with you three times by telephone since your crew of workers finished its work at our house. I told you on each occasion that the work your employees did here was absolutely terrible. Among the problems are that trees were pruned improperly and limbs were left hanging from them. The deep holes where trees were removed have been left in the lawn; garbage and leftover supplies have not been removed; our hedge was not pruned; and we are finding cigarette butts everywhere. ❶ Each time I speak with you, you tell me

> **ANALYSIS**
> ❶ This letter describes what is wrong with the work that was done so that it is clear what must be done to remedy it. This is always a useful thing to do.

that your crew will come here within the next day or two to fix the problems, but each time nothing happens.

In our last telephone call three days ago, you said, "I know you are dissatisfied with how we left your property and we will honor our responsibility to make it right." **2** I took this seriously and made note of it.

If your employees don't come here this week to repair the damage they have done and finish the work properly, I'm going to hire another garden company to make things right and speak with a lawyer about what actions would be appropriate with regard to your work. **3** You can be sure that I don't intend to stand for what your company has done, especially since you have told me yourself that you recognize what you must do to fix things.

Sincerely,

John R. Rae

15. Letter to dry cleaner who ruined jacket:

This is the kind of matter that is perfect for a small claims court, since Mr. Foster has evidence of what the dry cleaner did and there is too little money involved to hire a lawyer. In most instances, it will not be necessary to file a lawsuit, since most cleaners that damage your property would rather respond to a letter like this than have to send someone to small claims court to defend the case and probably lose. The threat to go to the small claims court is not made in this initial letter, but could be made in a subsequent letter. This letter follows a telephone call that obviously was not taken seriously.

October 23, 2002

Ms. Jane D. Smith
Smith Family Cleaners
227 Church Street
Madison, Wisconsin 00000

Dear Ms. Smith:

I am writing to confirm my demand that you pay me for the suede jacket that I brought to be cleaned at your store last week and was returned to me irrevocably damaged.

The suede jacket I brought to you to clean last week was brand-new. I explained to you that the only reason I was having it cleaned was that I had attended a meeting where there had been heavy smoking and the smell of the smoke lingered in the jacket. The man behind the counter, whose name I don't know, told me he understood why I was having the new jacket cleaned and assured me that it would be no problem. I picked the jacket up last Friday to find that the leather had been badly discolored and the lining had been shrunk.

I am enclosing a copy of my credit card receipt for the jacket, as well as a copy of the cleaning bill. I expect to be reimbursed for both expenses. As you can see, I purchased the jacket only 15 days before I took it to your store to be cleaned. I bought it on sale for only $85 and it was the last of its kind. Because of your error, I will undoubtedly have to pay more for another jacket. Please forward payment to me in the

amount of $140 immediately so that I can begin my
search for a replacement.

Sincerely,

Wayne R. Foster

Enclosures ①

16. Letter to plumber who made defective repairs:

November 27, 2002

<u>Certified Mail</u>
<u>Return Receipt Requested</u>

Mr. William C. Martin
Martin Plumbing Co.
4012 Sharp Street
Miami, Florida 00000

Dear Mr. Martin:

Yesterday was the third day you promised to come to our house to repair the leak coming from the new sink you installed in our bathroom. It has now been three weeks since you installed the sink, and we are still finding water underneath it every time we go into the bathroom. This is a dangerous condition—it would be easy for someone to slip on the wet floor—and it is worsening. I am sure you would not like to see someone injured as a result of this condition. ❶

> **ANALYSIS**
> ❶ Any time a condition caused by bad work is dangerous or damaging, it is useful to mention that in your letter. People who receive letters that say things like this are concerned that if they do not fix the problem promptly, they may be responsible for more serious harm.

When I spoke with you this past Wednesday night at your home, you said, "I am really sorry that I didn't come to your house, but I absolutely will be there on Friday to fix the sink. I know I am responsible for it and I'm not running away." ② Even though you said this to me, and promised for the third time to come on Friday, you didn't show up. If the sink is not fixed by December 7, I am going to be forced to hire another plumber to repair the work and bill you for that expense. ③

Please call me immediately after you receive this letter and tell me precisely when you will be here to fix the sink.

Sincerely,

Beryl A. Black

ANALYSIS

② This letter uses a quote from Mr. Martin in which he admits responsibility for the problem. When you use a quote like this, you are showing the other person that you are keeping careful records.

ANALYSIS

③ Telling someone who has done defective work for you that you will be forced to hire someone else to correct it is always powerful. Anybody with any sense realizes that if someone is hired to correct his work, he or she will be witness to what was done incorrectly.

17. Letter to tax preparation service about failures of tax preparer:

July 20, 2003

<u>Certified Mail</u>
<u>Return Receipt Requested</u>

Mark W. Davis, C.P.A.
Managing Partner
Davis Tax Services
2600 Beetle Street
Cherry Hill, New Jersey 00000

Dear Mr. Davis:

I am writing to you because my husband and I have been unable to resolve the problem we are having with Mr. Caraway. Mr. Caraway was assigned by your office to be the tax preparer for our 2002 tax returns.

On April 4, 2003, my husband and I visited your office on Beetle Street to have our tax returns for 2002 prepared for us. We were assigned to Mr. Caraway and were told to return to the office the next day with the relevant paperwork. We got all the papers together and returned with them the next day. We met with Mr. Caraway and he prepared our 2002 tax returns. Mr. Caraway told us that we would receive a refund of $817.43 as soon as the IRS processed the federal return. We were also supposed to receive a state refund of $87.41.

Our refunds never arrived, and on July 12, 2003, we received a letter from the IRS saying that we had to come to a conference at the federal office building in about three weeks. When we called your office and asked the person who answered the telephone what to do, she said we should speak with Mr. Caraway and he would assist us with the conference. We have tele-phoned Mr. Caraway about five times and only spoken with him for a minute or two several days ago. Mr. Caraway said it wasn't necessary for him to go to the conference and we should go and answer all the ques-tions ourselves. This isn't what we agreed to with your business when we hired you to prepare our tax returns, and we are not going to go to what is appar-ently an audit without professional assistance.

Since Mr. Caraway prepared our tax returns and is fully familiar with this matter, we would prefer to have him attend the IRS conference with us. If there is some reason why he cannot attend, we expect you to designate a replacement for Mr. Caraway who will be familiar with our situation. The conference with the IRS is coming up in less than two weeks, on August 2, 2003. ①

Please let us hear from you promptly so that we can know what is going to happen.

Sincerely,

Ruby C. Taft

cc: Mr. Reuben H. Caraway ②

18. Letter to mason regarding defective work:

October 19, 2002

Certified Mail ❶
Return Receipt Requested

Mr. Wilbur Blackburn
2341 Meadowbrook Drive
Chicago, Illinois 00000

> **ANALYSIS**
>
> ❶ This is the sort of letter where certified mail, return receipt requested, is very useful. The Jacksons have tried to resolve this matter with Mr. Blackburn, but he refuses to correct it and takes the position that the work is satisfactory. It is time for a letter that will get Mr. Blackburn moving in the right direction.

Dear Mr. Blackburn:

We have discussed the brickwork you did at our house on at least three occasions, and we are unable to agree about it. The work you did is completely unsatisfactory and we need to have it fixed, either by you or another mason. The bricks are crooked, as anyone can see, and the grout between the bricks is pointed up very badly. The finished product appears to be a very sloppy job. You have refused to fix the work and told us that you believe it is satisfactory. We cannot accept this.

We are prepared to file a lawsuit for the cost of correcting this work. However, I have a suggestion to make before we do that. My suggestion is that we agree on a competent mason and ask him to look over the work you did. If that mason thinks that your work is satisfactory, we will pay his bill and that will be the end of the matter. If he feels your work is not satisfactory, you will pay his fee and correct your work or pay him to correct it. ❷

Please let me know in the next few days if this suggestion is acceptable. If not, my wife and I will proceed with our suit. ❸

Sincerely,

Emily Y. Jackson
Andrew J. Jackson

19. Letter to contractor who built faulty addition to house:

November 23, 2003

<u>Certified Mail</u>
<u>Return Receipt Requested</u>

Mr. Adam Smithline
Perfect Home Improvements, Inc.
1253 Normandy Way
Albany, New York 00000

Dear Mr. Smithline:

The expensive addition you built on our house is a great disappointment. I have spoken with you on numerous occasions about its defects, and I will confirm them in this letter.

The addition was completed and we received a certificate of occupancy on November 9, 2003. Aside from a punch list of minor items (missing door hardware, screens for some of the windows, an air filter for the heat pump, additional grab bars in the bathroom, touch-up painting, and a new cover for the thermostat) that had nothing to do with the structure itself, the addition was complete on that date.

Beginning only four days later, on November 13, 2003, difficulties with the addition became noticeable. The roof of the addition leaked where it was connected to the original house, as well as at the top of the large picture window. (The gutters on the addition were apparently sloped away from the downspout, so that water accumulates in them and runs over the gutters rather than down the downspout.) The heating and air conditioning for the addition are not nearly adequate, and the addition is now far too cold to use. Furthermore, the trim work and the flooring are sloppy, and parts of each of them are coming loose. The tile in the bathroom was not carefully installed, and it is chipping.

Since you were the general contractor for this work and all of the subcontractors were hired by you, you are responsible for every bit of it. ❶ The short of it is that this addition was not constructed in a workmanlike ❷ fashion and many repairs are necessary. We have no intention of making final payment to you at this time, and we will not do so until all the necessary repairs are made

ANALYSIS

❶ When a general contract is used, the general contractor is responsible for the work of all of the subcontractors. This is a different situation from what is known as "construction management." In construction management all subcontractors are hired by the owner and there is a separate, different contract with each of them. Most additions are done by general contractors, which is certainly desirable from an owner's point of view because the owner then has only one party he or she needs to look to to correct defects.

and the punch list items are also properly completed.

We would like to resolve this matter amicably with you. We are aware that the items that need to be repaired or replaced will be somewhat costly, but they are definitely items that must be corrected. In the hope that we will be able to resolve this matter, we have not pursued any legal action regarding the addition and we have not even requested a qualified builder to inspect the work that was done. ❸

We would like to schedule a meeting with you immediately so that we may do our best to agree upon the repair and replacement work that is necessary and get it done. I would appreciate hearing from you promptly to arrange such a meeting.

Sincerely,

John J. Blatchford

20. Letter to contractor who installed hazardous garage door:

August 30, 2003

<u>Certified Mail</u>
<u>Return Receipt Requested</u>

Mr. Robert G. Moore
1000 Montebello Drive
Seattle, Washington 00000

Dear Mr. Moore:

Your newly completed installation of an electric garage door at our house is not satisfactory. The unit does not contain a safety device to assure that the door doesn't close on a person or pet. This is a hazardous

❶ condition, and we are leaving the electric door unplugged until you fix it. I have been told that it is against the law for anyone to install an electric garage door without a safety

> **ANALYSIS**
>
> ❶ This letter uses the buzzword "hazardous," and it explains why what the contractor has done is hazardous. It should not be necessary to say anything further to get the door fixed.

device to make sure it does not close on someone. ②
I am going to verify this information if I do not hear
from you in the next several days that you are coming to fix it.

Sincerely,

Susan N. Porter

ANALYSIS

② Ms. Porter has given Mr. Moore an extra incentive to repair the door by letting him know that she has been told that a law may be violated if there is no safety device. There is such a law in many places. You should note that Ms. Porter has proceeded properly by mentioning the information she has received regarding the law. She has not threatened anything, but her letter makes her point very well.

ANALYSIS

Note that Ms. Porter is complaining about a defective installation job, not about a defective product. Mr. Moore has failed to install a safety device, which is often a separate device from the electric mechanism that raises and lowers the doors. Many older electric garage doors have a mechanism at the bottom that causes the door to go back up when it strikes something. Many newer garage doors have an electric eye beam across the bottom of the opening, which prevents the doors from closing when the beam is interrupted. This is a matter for which the installer is responsible.

21. Letter to caterer that botched up "Sweet Sixteen" party:

If Mr. Bromley does not return the Bouviers' money, and a lawsuit is instituted, there will definitely be a legal question of whether they are entitled to damages beyond what they paid. It is often legally difficult or impossible to recover damages beyond what you paid for something. Nevertheless, the Bouviers have a good faith basis for trying to recover such damages, and they can tell Mr. Bromley that they will do so unless he returns the money they have paid.

April 25, 2004

Certified Mail
Return Receipt Requested

Mr. Wilford Bromley
Bromley Caterers
926 Medallion Road
Stewartstown, Maine 00000

Dear Mr. Bromley:

The Sweet 16 party for our daughter, which you catered at our home last Saturday evening, was absolutely disgraceful. Your company failed in almost every respect to provide the food and service for which we paid $50 per person for 90 people.

Where shall I begin? The tent you erected at the side of our house was much too small for the number of people you knew would attend. In addition, anyone with any sense would realize that in the month of April, heaters would be required inside the tent. The tent was freezing during most of the party.

As for the food, it failed in every respect to measure up to what was promised. There were numerous substitutions for dishes that we had agreed on, and the amount of food was much less than needed for a party of 90 people. In addition, the hot food was barely lukewarm when it was served.

Instead of providing six servers, as we had agreed on, there were only four. The service was also very poor and very slow. ❶

My husband and I have considered this matter carefully and decided to demand the return of all monies we paid to you for this party. We have paid you $4,500 plus $650 for extras of which you advised us at the last minute.

ANALYSIS

❶ Anytime you demand reimbursement of money you have paid for something that was not adequately provided, be sure to specify precisely how the goods or services were defective or lacking.

Obviously the return of our money will not cure the damage you have done to our family. We suffered great embarrassment in front of our closest friends and relatives and our daughter's schoolmates. No amount of money will make up for that.

I am writing this letter in order to make one attempt to settle the matter without lawyers. We do not intend to compromise this matter with you, and we are not interested in discussing it. If we receive a check in the amount of $5,150 within the next week, we will consider the matter closed. If not, we will discuss with our lawyer the proper way to proceed against you to recover not only the money we paid to you but also whatever damages we are entitled to for the harm you have done to our family. **2**

Sincerely,

Catherine M. Bouvier

22. Letter to company trying to enforce a contract you have canceled:

May 15, 2003

<u>Certified Mail</u>
<u>Return Receipt Requested</u>

Mr. Mark Smith
Smith Building Contractors
237 Maple Lane
Pittsburgh, Pennsylvania 00000

Dear Mr. Smith:

I have told you on several occasions, and I repeat here, that my wife and I do not intend to use your company for the construction work we have planned. When we signed a contract with you two months ago we made it clear that we were not interested in entering into the agreement unless work could begin in the next two weeks and finish in six weeks. It has now been five weeks since we signed the contract and the work still has not started. ①

In case there is any doubt about it, I am specifically advising you by this letter that you are not to enter our property under any circumstances. There is nothing on our property that belongs to your company, and we do not wish to be disturbed by this matter any longer.

If you have any further concerns about this matter, please put them in writing and do not call us. We will review the matter with a lawyer if that is necessary. ②

Sincerely,

Jonathan S. Smith

23. Letter to utility company that is not providing adequate service:

April 3, 2003

Certified Mail
Return Receipt Requested

Customer Relations Manager ❶
Allstate Energy Services, Inc.
2000 Energy Parkway
Edison, New Jersey 00000

Re: 5162 Ivory Drive ❷
Edison, New Jersey 00000
Account No. 000000000

Dear Sir or Madam:

Our electrical service has been disrupted five times in the past month. On one of those occasions we went without electric power for two and a half days. The servicemen from your company tell us that the difficulty is that our overhead power line passes through the woods behind our house and dead branches keep falling on the wire. We have asked to have all the dead branches removed, but each time the servicemen come, they repair the wire but do nothing about the branches. We see trucks in this neighborhood that cut branches hanging over wires, but no one has done this in the woods behind our house. ❸

We are not receiving electrical service in the appropriate manner. I would not be writing if this happened once in a while, but it is happening constantly and we are suffering considerable difficulty because of it. One of the occupants of our house is ill, and besides her being unable to tolerate the loss of heat and hot water for long periods of time, she relies on special medical equipment that requires electric power to run. ❹

Please take the necessary steps to arrange to have the dead branches that interfere with our power line removed. I would appreciate it if you would notify me when this will occur.

Sincerely,

Justin B. Downs

24. Letter to primary care physician who will not return phone calls:

Writing to your primary care physician is always difficult because you want your relationship with your physician to be as good as possible. You have no choice, however, when you are having a serious medical difficulty and are unable to get a response. When you must write such letters, stick to the facts, make your condition clear, and tell the doctor exactly what you want to happen.

March 1, 2003

Via Fax: 000-000-0000 ❶

James L. Livingston, M.D.
Glenmont Medical Center
216 Green Street
Glenmont, Maryland 00000

Dear Dr. Livingston:

I have been trying for over a week to get in touch with you by telephone. The reason I called is that the prescription you gave me on February 19, 2003, when I visited your office, is not working. Each time I tried to take it I got severe stomach upset.

> **ANALYSIS**
> ❶ This letter is sent by facsimile because it obviously needs to be received by Dr. Livingston immediately. There will not be a problem of proving delivery in an instance such as this, and even where there might be one, most fax machines have a method for printing a verification of what was sent.

I visited you the first time for pain in my lower back on December 16, 2002. I told you at that time that the pain started in September and by December it was severe and preventing me from sleeping and from doing some of my regular work. You recommended hot baths and Tylenol, and I followed your advice. When I returned on February 19, 2003, I told you that the pain was much worse and the hot baths and Tylenol were not relieving it. You gave me prescriptions for a muscle relaxer and a stronger pain medication. The muscle relaxer makes me sleepy. The pain-killer causes me to have a severe upset stomach, but it doesn't help with the pain.

For the past week I have telephoned you every day to discuss this matter, but I can't reach you. I need to speak with you immediately because these drugs are not doing what they are supposed to do and my severe back pain is unbearable nearly all the time. I want to discuss with you all the possibilities for my treatment. **2**

Please telephone me immediately so that we can discuss this matter. I realize that you are extremely busy, but this condition has become unbearable for me. I will come to another appointment at your

convenience. You can reach me at work during the
day at 555-123-4567 and in the evenings after 6:00
P.M. at my home at 555-123-0387. I would appreciate
it if you called me immediately, as I need medical care
urgently. ❸

Sincerely,

William C. Jones

25. Letter to HMO or other health care provider requesting reimbursement for medical expenses:

March 23, 2003

<u>Certified Mail</u>
<u>Return Receipt Requested</u>

Ms. Sarah R. Spiegel
Carefree Insurance Company
7928 Blackburn Road
Austin, Texas 00000

Dear Ms. Spiegel:

I have telephoned you twice and requested reimbursement for medical services to which I am entitled under my contract, but you have not forwarded payment to me.

On February 5, 2003, I required emergency medical treatment for a broken leg that resulted from a skiing accident in Vermont. Since I was away from home at the time, I needed to pay the clinic and orthopedic surgeon myself, and I have requested reimbursement in accordance with the contract with Carefree Insurance Company.

The "Covered Persons Agreement," which is my contract with your company, states in Section 17b(ii): "payment for emergency care will be made at normal and reasonable rates, provided that this company is given advance notice of the necessity for such care, unless such notice is not reasonably possible due to the circumstances of the emergency." ➊ The circumstances of this emergency were that I needed immediate medical care and was taken by ambulance in extreme pain to the nearest available treatment facility. Once I had been treated and stabilized at that facility, I immediately returned home. All later treatment was provided through your company in the usual manner.

I forwarded the bills for the clinic and orthopedic surgeon to you on February 10, 2003. Both bills were marked "Paid in full."

On March 11, 2003, I telephoned you to inquire why I had not been reimbursed.

ANALYSIS

➊ By quoting directly from her contract with Carefree Insurance Company, Ms. Shoemaker does two things. First, she is showing the company that she is a careful person who knows what she is entitled to under her contract. Second, the company knows that if it does not pay her, Ms. Shoemaker will tell the State Health Claims Office that a specific provision of her contract is being violated and the insurance company has been advised of that. This will be bad for the insurance company if the State Health Claims Office gets into the matter. In most situations, this sort of letter will get you your check.

On March 16, 2003, I made a second telephone call for the same purpose. ②

As of today, the bills remain unpaid.

Your company is in violation of its contract with me. I intend to review the matter with the State Health Claims Office unless I receive payment from you no later than April 2. ③

Sincerely,

Bernelle D. Shoemaker

ANALYSIS

② By reviewing all of the facts, including the reason why she could not give the insurance company advance notice, Ms. Shoemaker has destroyed the insurance company's ability to continue not paying her claim by saying that it does not have the facts straight.

ANALYSIS

③ This letter is an exception to the general rule that you should not threaten to take action involving a public agency in order to settle a private claim. The reason for the exception is that the contract in this instance provides for this method of resolving disputes with the health care provider.

ANALYSIS

When you write such letters, be certain that you have carefully reviewed your contract. Follow its provisions carefully so that the provider will not be able to avoid your claim by stating that you broke the contract. The state health claims office or other state agency responsible for reviewing these matters, should you need to contact a third party, will be familiar with the provisions of your contract.

26. Letter to HMO regarding need for extensive medical care:

April 10, 2003

<u>Certified Mail</u>
<u>Return Receipt Requested</u>

Ms. Sarah R. Spiegel
Carefree Insurance Company
7928 Blackburn Road
Austin, Texas 00000

Dear Ms. Spiegel:

I am very concerned about the further degeneration of my left hip and the refusal of Carefree Insurance Company to provide me with medical care that is necessary for it. Let me review for you the facts of this matter to date:

On January 10, 2002, I had an appointment with Dr. Alfred James, my primary care physician. I advised Dr. James that I had considerable pain and motion limitations in my left hip. He examined me and confirmed this. Dr. James has been aware of the automobile injury I suffered in 1994 and my general arthritic condition, particularly in this hip, since 1996. On January 10, Dr. James prescribed an anti-inflammatory drug for my condition and recommended periodic use of Advil. I obeyed Dr. James's instructions.

On March 8, 2002, I had another appointment with Dr. James, and I advised him that my condition had not improved. In fact, examination showed that my pain and motion restriction had worsened in the two-month period. With the exception of a simple X ray taken in Dr. James's office at that time, I was not scheduled for any testing at this appointment.

In April, May, and June 2002, I telephoned Dr. James on numerous occasions and advised him each time that my situation had worsened. I requested several times that I be sent for further tests to determine whether surgery or some other form of medical assistance was necessary. Dr. James never scheduled any further tests and never referred me to a specialist.

In November 2002, at my own expense, I visited Dr. Sterling Stewart, an orthopedic surgeon. He arranged for me to have a CT scan examination, which was also done at my expense. After spending about $1,000 of my own money, I learned that my left hip has degenerated to the point where prosthetic replacement is absolutely necessary. ①

On December 12, 2002, I told Dr. James that I had received this information, and I sent him copies of the CT scan report and Dr. Stewart's note of opinion. I told Dr. James that I felt this matter had to be pursued immediately so that I would receive the medical treatment I require for my condition.

On February 27, 2003, I spoke with Dr. James, and he advised me that he has provided you with all information necessary to determine what further medical care I should receive.

It's clear from my contract with you that I am entitled under these circumstances to be referred to an orthopedic surgeon for replacement of my left hip with an appropriate prosthetic device, as well as all testing, medication, and other medical needs associated with that. I would like to use Dr. Stewart for that purpose, although he is not listed in your directory of specialists. Had you taken appropriate steps regarding this matter in a timely fashion, I would not have needed to consult Dr. Stewart in the first place. I should not have

---

ANALYSIS

① Mr. Fielding arranged a private consultation and test at his own expense; by doing so, he obtained information that is useful in persuading his HMO to provide further care. Unfortunately, it is sometimes necessary to spend money in order to accomplish things to which you are entitled. Ideally, Mr. Fielding will be reimbursed for this expense; regardless, his decision to incur it was certainly a reasonable one. Dr. Stewart's information makes the history of events in this matter much stronger for Mr. Fielding's position that the HMO must provide him with the medical care he seeks.

to face the expense and inconvenience of starting the diagnostic process all over again. I expect you to approve this medical procedure and to reimburse me for the expenses I have incurred so far. ❷

I must have your decision regarding my future care promptly. If I do not receive it by the end of this week, I will be forced to contact the state health claims office and proceed in the manner described in my contract. I certainly hope that will not be necessary.

Sincerely,

Jonathan S. Fielding

ANALYSIS

❷ Whenever you write to an insurance company or other health care provider, refer to your contract, as Mr. Fielding has done. This shows the health care provider that you are a conscientious person and have familiarized yourself with your rights and its obligations. It also tells any other party who may review the matter where to look in order to resolve it in your favor.

27. Letter to HMO demanding referral to specialist:

March 26, 2003

<u>Certified Mail</u>
<u>Return Receipt Requested</u>

Ms. Sarah D. Eldridge
Gateway Insurance Network
3333 Washington Boulevard
Seattle, Washington 00000

Dear Ms. Eldridge:

As you know from my earlier letters, I believe that your company has acted irresponsibly and is in violation of your contract with me by denying me the opportunity to be referred to a specialist for the stomach difficulties I have had for nearly six months. I have reviewed this matter several times with my primary care physician, Dr. Edmund Willoughby, and he is apparently unable to do anything to assist me.

I am advising you that I have notified the State Health

Claims Arbitration Bureau of the difficulty I am having receiving proper medical care for my serious condition. My provider agreement with your company indicates that this is the appropriate thing for me to do when I am unable to resolve this sort of difficulty with your company. Your company will be formally notified that I have filed this complaint, and a hearing will be scheduled. The arbitration bureau will request my relevant records from Dr. Willoughby and your company in the very near future.

I am sorry that the matter has come to this, but I am in bad need of further medical treatment for my stomach condition. I hope that the hearing will be scheduled very soon, since I am suffering considerable pain and discomfort as I wait for further treatment.

Sincerely,

Patricia N. Andrews

This letter threatens nothing. It advises the HMO that you have used the procedure indicated in its provider agreement with you and followed the instructions of the state official. The HMO must now make a judgment with regard to this matter with full knowledge that the state will be looking over its shoulder.

In a situation like this, you should be certain to get all of your materials about your illness together in case there is a hearing. In order to show that your health care provider has not done what it is supposed to do, you must create a paper trail: a series of written materials such as letters that show what the health care provider failed to do and, also, that it knew of its failure.

Very often there will be no hearing because the HMO will do what you want in order to avoid being told by the state that it has failed to meet its obligations. HMOs are controlled in various ways in every state, and they don't want to risk losing their state approvals. There is an old legal saying that "the best way to avoid a contest is to prepare for it." This is certainly true of medical expense reimbursement difficulties.

28. Letter to HMO regarding need to go outside of network:

February 2, 2004

Via Federal Express ①

Ms. Sarah R. Spiegel
Carefree Insurance Company
7928 Blackburn Road
Austin, Texas 00000

Dear Ms. Spiegel:

I am writing to you regarding my daughter's urgent need for specialized medical care.

ANALYSIS

① This is a take-no-prisoners letter to an HMO. The Snyders' daughter's need for medical care is critical, and the HMO is not providing it. When you write such a letter, you must do so in the clearest and most forceful terms possible. This letter makes the history of the matter absolutely clear and accurate. Federal Express is essential in this case because the letter must arrive the following day. Obviously that will provide proof of delivery as well.

My daughter, Stacy, is a covered person under our contract of July 15, 2003. Therefore, she is entitled to qualified specialized care for her condition in accordance with Part 7 of the contract between us. You have not questioned this, but the specialized care you have offered to make available is not adequate for my daughter's needs.

In November 2003 my daughter began to experience extreme loss of energy and other symptoms consistent with a thyroid disorder. Her primary care physician, Dr. Leopold H. Skidmore, arranged for her to have comprehensive blood and urine tests. The blood tests revealed that she has hypothyroidism, which means that she does not produce sufficient thyroxine. Other examinations and tests ultimately showed that my daughter has cancer of the thyroid and requires immediate surgical intervention and further treatment.

We understand from a great many conversations with physicians and others that my daughter needs two kinds of specialists: a surgeon with experience in removal of the thyroid gland and an endocrinologist for follow-up treatment. Follow-up treatment will ensure that the cancer has not spread and help her doctors determine Stacy's need for drugs to replace the hormones she will no longer be producing.

Unfortunately, the network of specialists you make available to covered persons in your HMO does not include a suitable specialist of either type. The surgeon that has been recommended by Dr. Skidmore has almost no experience in the removal of thyroid glands and certainly is nowhere near a qualified surgeon for this purpose. In addition, Dr. Skidmore has told us that you have requested him to provide the follow-up treatment for our daughter. Dr. Skidmore is not an endocrinologist and has none of the experience our daughter needs.

We have carefully reviewed the covered persons agreement that is our contract with you. It indicates that covered persons will be permitted to go out of your network of doctors when you do not have in your network specialists who are qualified to provide the medical care that is needed. There is no question that this is the situation in this case. Since time is critical in this matter, our daughter needs to consult and make arrangements with these two specialists immediately.

We have consulted with experts in this matter because we are so deeply concerned about it. Dr. Milton H. Vorhees, a surgeon with extensive experience in the removal of thyroid glands, has advised us that this is a matter for an experienced surgeon and that follow-up care by an experienced endocrinologist is essential. At Dr. Vorhees's suggestion we consulted with Dr. Cynthia H. Clayborne, an endocrinologist. She confirmed what Dr. Vorhees told us. **2**

ANALYSIS

2 This letter introduces outside experts by naming Drs. Vorhees and Clayborne, whom the Snyders have consulted. This is the sort of situation where such consultation is absolutely necessary in order to obtain what is required.

Our daughter's condition and her need for immediate medical care do not allow us time to debate this matter with you. We understand from your literature the procedure for state review. ❸ We will begin that procedure immediately unless you indicate to us within the next 72 hours that we may use the two necessary specialists out of your network.

ANALYSIS

❸ The Snyders indicate that they will be following the procedure outlined by the HMO in seeking state review of the matter. This leaves no doubt that they are familiar with their contract and that they intend to enforce its provisions.

We want to emphasize that if you insist that our daughter's surgery be done by a surgeon without experience in the removal of thyroid glands and if you insist that her follow-up care be done by her primary care physician instead of an experienced endocrinologist, it will be our position that you have breached your contract with us. In addition, the medical care you would provide to our daughter would not satisfy prevailing medical standards. ❹ Our consultations with Drs. Vorhees and Clayborne convince us that this is the case, and we will not accept substandard medical care for our daughter in this life-threatening situation. Since they have already familiarized themselves with our daughter's case, we expect to use Drs. Vorhees and

ANALYSIS

❹ This letter introduces the matter of a possible medical malpractice claim by saying that the care being offered by the HMO does not meet prevailing medical standards. When you are faced with a matter this critical, use your buzzwords. If I were the HMO's lawyer and reviewed this letter, I would advise my client to think hard (and fast!) about providing the medical care the Snyders demand for their daughter.

Clayborne for her treatment. We are advising you in no uncertain terms that if you insist on following this procedure, we will hold you responsible for failure to provide our daughter with care that meets prevailing medical standards.

We expect to hear from you within 72 hours.

Sincerely,

Matthew R. Snyder

29. Letter to health care provider demanding that it provide a medically necessary device:

October 19, 2003

<u>Certified Mail</u> **①**
<u>Return Receipt Requested</u>

Mr. Carlos Bendaras
Supervisor
Carefree Insurance Company
7928 Blackburn Road
Austin, Texas 00000

Re: Member No. 000-00-0000

Dear Mr. Bendaras:

I am a member of your HMO. I write concerning my
acute medical need for an electric wheelchair. I have
been advised by my general physician, Dr. Wilma C.
Rattle, that you have authorized me to obtain a manual
wheelchair, but not an electric one. Unfortunately, a
manual wheelchair will not serve my medical needs.

A manual wheelchair will be unsatisfactory for me for several reasons. First, I experience extreme pain in my arms and upper back when I move a manual wheelchair. Second, I cannot attend to the requirements of my life at home and my limited life outside my home without the mobility that is provided by an electric wheelchair. I have reviewed this matter carefully with the three medical practitioners with whom I deal concerning my physical disability. I am enclosing precise information from each of them concerning this matter:

(1) You find enclosed a report of Dr. Seymour Gladding, my orthopedic surgeon, which clearly indicates that I am not able to move around in a manual wheelchair to any satisfactory extent. **2**

ANALYSIS

2 Whenever you are fighting to get something expensive you need for medical purposes, get your documentation in order before you begin your letter writing. There is nothing more useful in such a matter than good documentation. In this case, Mr. Wallace has obtained reports from two physicians and his physical therapist.

(2) You will also find enclosed a report of Dr. Rattle, advising me to limit my use of a manual wheelchair to avoid stressing the muscles that have been injured in my arms and back. **3**

(3) You will also find enclosed a report of my physical therapist, Ms. Dora H. Hunting, which deals precisely with the assistance I need to move about

reasonably. As you can see from Ms. Hunting's report, she has actually tested my abilities in a manual wheelchair and found them to be deficient. ④

Please review this matter carefully and let me hear from you at your earliest convenience.

Sincerely,

Terrence C. Wallace

Enclosures

30. Letter to HMO requesting change in primary care physician:

July 8, 2003

Ms. Sarah R. Spiegel ①
Carefree Insurance Company
7928 Blackburn Road
Austin, Texas 00000

Dear Ms. Spiegel:

Since we joined your health maintenance organization
in 1998, the primary care physician for both my husband and me has been Dr. Peggy E. Smothers. We
have been generally satisfied with her services until
recently, when my husband developed high blood pressure, which requires medication. My husband needs to
consult Dr. Smothers often to have his medication
adjusted.

The problem we are having with Dr. Smothers is that
she is almost impossible to reach by telephone to
schedule appointments to check my husband's condition and determine whether he is taking the correct

ANALYSIS

① This letter was sent by
regular mail, since the
HMO will either acknowl-
edge the Stewarts' request
to change the general physician or speak with Dr.
Smothers about being more
attentive. This is not the
sort of situation where great
force is necessary.

dosage of his medicine. The kind of medicine my husband is taking requires him to consult often with his doctor because the high dosage he is taking sometimes causes side effects. We are certainly entitled to have a general physician who is accessible enough to properly monitor my husband's health. ❷

We request that you review this matter immediately and designate a new general physician for us who will have the time to schedule the necessary appointments with my husband and follow his dosage carefully. ❸ We are sorry that this is necessary because we like Dr. Smothers and wish it were possible to continue with her care.

Sincerely,

Michelle T. Stewart

31. Letter to physician regarding medical care for incompetent son:

January 23, 2003

Paul W. Brown, M.D.
Brown & Associates, P.A.
29 W. Read Street
Johnstown, Pennsylvania 00000

Dear Dr. Brown:

My husband and I continue to be greatly concerned about the medical care our son Jonas, age 22, is receiving. We realize that Jonas's mental incompetence makes him a difficult patient, but we understood that our HMO designated you to be his doctor because of your experience in this regard. I am writing to confirm two specific concerns regarding Jonas that my husband and I have expressed to you several times. ❶

Our first concern is that Jonas does not have a very good sense of balance. He frequently loses his balance and has fallen and injured himself more than once. We know that there are a variety of tests that could shed some light on this matter, and we have repeatedly requested that Jonas be tested. ❷

The second problem is that Jonas obviously has some serious allergies to foods. Jonas has never had complete testing for this, and now his food allergies seem to be getting worse. Seafood seems to be the worst irritant, and the last time he ate it he had difficulty breathing. My husband and I are aware that there are comprehensive tests for food allergies, and we believe that Jonas badly needs them.

I am requesting that you advise us as promptly as possible whether Jonas will be tested with regard to his balance and allergy problems. Our hope is that these tests will be done in the very near future. If we experience further difficulty regarding this matter, we will pursue it with our HMO, but we certainly hope that that will not be necessary. ❸

We look forward to hearing from you.

Sincerely,

Anna M. Tonbridge,
Guardian for Jonas Tonbridge

ANALYSIS

❷ Mrs. Tonbridge has said enough to make it clear that the matter is an important one. Her son is losing his balance and falling and reacting adversely to certain foods. Whenever you try to get medical care that is not being provided, you should make it clear to everyone to whom you write that adverse consequences are happening.

ANALYSIS

❸ This is a letter demanding particular action with respect to Jonas. Since it is a letter to the designated physician, it is the Tonbridges' first attempt to obtain what is needed. When you deal with a problem regarding medical care that is not being provided, you should always give the physician the first opportunity to see if the matter can be resolved. If it cannot, the Tonbridges can pursue the matter with the HMO directly.

32. Letter to HMO that claims overpayment:

May 25, 2003

Ms. Jane C. Baldwin
Carefree Health Management Company
7928 Blackburn Road
Austin, Texas 00000

Re: Account No. 000-00-0000

Dear Ms. Baldwin:

I have received your letter of May 15, 2003, requesting me to refund money for an overpayment by your HMO. I regret that there has been some misunderstanding, but I do not owe you any money for overpayment for tests.

As you can see from the records of my general physician, Dr. Bernard Sharpless, I have had a seriously inflamed gallbladder for at least five months. I was referred to the first specialist, Dr. William Blakesmyer, about four weeks after the difficulty first began. Dr. Blakesmyer performed several tests that he deemed necessary and, when the results were in, recommended that I have surgery.

I then saw Dr. Elaine Snodgrass to obtain a second opinion regarding the matter of surgery, which is an approved course of action according to your handbook. Dr. Snodgrass conducted a number of tests, one or two of which were repeats of tests Dr. Sharpless had performed. Dr. Snodgrass explained to me that she wanted certain things to be retested so that she could see if there had been any change in my condition. I am not a doctor, but this sounds reasonable to me. ①

ANALYSIS

① Ms. Snyder has explained in this letter why a second opinion was required in this instance and why additional testing, including some repeat testing, was necessary. She has made it clear that she will follow the review procedure of the HMO, including state agency review if necessary.

I do not see how a second opinion could be useful to a member of an HMO unless the second doctor is able to give whatever tests she feels are necessary. This is exactly what occurred in this instance, and nothing that was done was excessive. ②

ANALYSIS

② Just as with any claim by you for medical services or expenses from an HMO, you should fully document any refusal by the HMO to pay for medical services already rendered.

No one who is covered by an HMO or any other health insurer should be penalized in any way for asserting his or her position in this fashion.

As you can see, I do not owe your HMO any money. I hope you will be able to sort this matter out with the accounting department so that my husband and I no longer receive bills from that department. If this does not occur, I am prepared to follow the full review procedure set forth in my contract, including state agency review.

Thank you in advance for your help with this matter.

Sincerely,

Mary S. Snyder

33. Letter to HMO that won't pay for service:

This is a situation that is known in insurance jargon as "unbundling." Insurance companies save money when certain services are more economical when those services are combined, or "bundled." In this case the delivery service and circumcision service were separated by several weeks, which surely cost the HMO extra money. Unfortunately, that was not possible in this instance.

This is a firm demand letter, but it is worded in a way that assumes that the HMO will be reasonable. Virtually every HMO has a review procedure for matters like this, and you should check the requirements of that procedure any time you have such a difficulty. HMOs do change their mind about matters of payment when presented with reasonable arguments, particularly arguments they would prefer members not make in front of state agencies.

July 8, 2003

<u>Certified Mail</u>
<u>Return Receipt Requested</u>

Mr. Jonathan C. Marks
Review Supervisor
Carefree Insurance Company
7928 Blackburn Road
Austin, Texas 00000

Dear Mr. Marks:

I am writing to ask that the matter of nonpayment
for my son's circumcision be reviewed.

My son was delivered at Sagamore General Hospital
on March 12, 2003. In reviewing the matter with
your HMO, I was told that the cost of his circumcision would be paid by the HMO, provided it was
done in the hospital within days of his birth. As
it turned out, this was not possible because my
son's platelet count was low at the time of his
birth and even a minor surgical procedure would
have risked his life. My son's platelet count
returned to normal only after several platelet
transfusions and hematological attention. Twelve
weeks after his birth my pediatrician assured
me that there was no longer a risk, so he was

circumcised shortly thereafter, on June 9, 2003. ❶

I have been told by your HMO that it will not pay for my son's circumcision. Obviously this was a matter in which my husband and I had no choice whatsoever. We would gladly have followed your rules to the letter, but surely we could not endanger our son by having him circumcised at a time when his platelet count was so low that any operation, no matter how minor, would have endangered his life. As members of your HMO, we feel that we are entitled to coverage for this very simple procedure that we had performed as soon as it was safe to do so.

I ask you to review this matter and do the fair and appropriate thing by providing us with reimbursement for the cost of our son's circumcision. I enclose a copy of the bill.

Sincerely,

Anna Morgan

Enclosure

34. First letter to HMO requesting tests prior to use of medication:

September 14, 2003

Mr. John H. Quackenbush ❶
Quick and Easy HMO
2525 Manor Boulevard
Kansas City, Kansas 00000

Re: Mr. and Mrs. Harris T.
    Bainbridge
    Contract No. XYZ0000

Dear Mr. Quackenbush:

My wife and I have requested on three occasions that you arrange a full battery of tests for our daughter, Katherine Bainbridge, to determine whether she should be using Ritalin as has been suggested by her homeroom teacher. We are aware that our daughter does get agitated from time to time in class, but we are not at all certain that she is hyperactive in a way that requires regular use of this serious drug. Our general physician, Dr. Henry H. Thomas, has advised us that it is your HMO's decision not to provide a full battery of tests under these circumstances, but simply to authorize the use of this drug on a trial basis. We understand from a number of very reliable people that this procedure is ill-advised. In addition to blood, urine, and some other physical tests, our daughter is in need of a psychiatric consultation for this purpose. We have reviewed our contract with you and it provides for these things when necessary.

We would appreciate hearing from you as promptly as possible, since this situation is a serious one for our family.

Sincerely,

Harris T. Bainbridge

35. Second letter to HMO requesting tests prior to use of medication:

The Bainbridges have turned up the heat.

September 20, 2003

<u>Certified Mail</u> **1**
<u>Return Receipt Requested</u>

Mr. John H. Quackenbush
Quick and Easy HMO
2525 Manor Boulevard
Kansas City, Kansas 00000

Re: Mr. and Mrs. Harris T.
      Bainbridge
      Contract No. XYZ0000

Dear Mr. Quackenbush:

I have received your response to my letter of
September 14, 2003, and needless to say my wife and
I are not satisfied with it. In fact, we have discussed
the matter with Mr. Ivan Sturnburg, our group care

ANALYSIS

1 This letter, which was sent by certified mail, return receipt requested, advises the HMO that the group spokesperson has become involved in the matter and that health difficulties for their daughter are beginning to occur.

representative with your HMO, and he is very surprised by your declination to provide this care for our daughter. Mr. Sturnburg has authorized us to tell you that he has reviewed the correspondence in this matter and does not deem your response to be appropriate or consistent with our contract.

This matter is beginning to have serious health consequences for our daughter, and we wish to see it resolved immediately. Therefore, please refer this letter and all earlier correspondence and records to your review committee, which our contract materials indicate is available to review decisions such as this. I would appreciate it if you could confirm that you have done so as promptly as possible. **2**

Sincerely,

Harris T. Bainbridge

ANALYSIS

2 This letter also advises the HMO that the Bainbridges wish to initiate the formal review procedure that is described in their contract.

ANALYSIS

If you belong to a group that is being provided medical care by an HMO or other provider and difficulties arise, contact the spokesperson for that group. Groups have leverage that individual members or insureds do not have because medical care providers don't want to lose large premiums because of one or two unsatisfactory experiences.

36. Third letter to HMO requesting tests prior to use of medication:

September 27, 2003

<u>Certified Mail</u>
<u>Return Receipt Requested</u>

Mr. John H. Quackenbush
Quick and Easy HMO
2525 Manor Boulevard
Kansas City, Kansas 00000

Re: Mr. and Mrs. Harris T. Bainbridge
    Contract No. XYZ0000

Dear Mr. Quackenbush:

We understand that the review committee has now reviewed the situation concerning our daughter's possible need for Ritalin and has upheld your HMO's initial decision not to provide comprehensive testing. This is obviously thoroughly unsatisfactory to us, and we cannot abide by your decision.

Accordingly, we have been in touch with the Kansas Insurance Department and requested Mr. George L.

Wary of that office to arrange for formal review of your decision in accordance with state law. **①** Mr. Wary advised us that we will receive notice of a hearing within the next 30 days, and he has requested that copies of all correspondence and medical records be forwarded to him before that date. We will forward to Mr. Wary all such materials in our possession, and we request that you do likewise. **②**

Since this is a matter involving the health and welfare of our daughter, we cannot accept your HMO's decision not to provide her with medical care to which we are clearly entitled. You should be aware that Katherine's health is declining as a result of this delay and her difficulties in school are increasing greatly. **③**

Sincerely,

Harris T. Bainbridge

cc: Mr. George L. Wary

37. Letter to HMO requesting additional physical therapy:

Before you write a letter like this, be sure to check your membership agreement or insurance policy to determine how much physical therapy you are entitled to receive. Special needs, including physical therapy and mental health care, are generally limited in health care provider agreements today.

December 4, 2003

Ms. Margaret Hope
Quick and Easy HMO
2525 Manor Boulevard
Kansas City, Kansas 00000

Re: Randall H. Jamison
    Member No. 000000000

Dear Ms. Hope:

I am a member of your HMO with the above membership number.

Several months ago I broke the tibia of my right leg and received medical treatment from Dr. John Holcum, an orthopedic surgeon who was recommended by my general physician, Dr. Sylvia Bennett. I am completely satisfied with the care I received from Dr. Holcum and my leg has been healing well.

Dr. Holcum recommended that I receive physical therapy two times a week at home until use of the leg returns to normal. I started the physical therapy about eight or ten weeks after the break was repaired, since by then my leg could bear most of my weight.

The physical therapist to whom Dr. Holcum referred me, Janice Eldridge, has advised me that her company has only received approval for six visits for my treatment. This will obviously not be sufficient, and I am writing to request that you provide Ms. Eldridge's company with further authorization. Dr. Holcum has indicated that I will need at least six weeks, and possibly eight or ten weeks, of physical therapy to return to the normal use of my leg. This is obviously of great importance to me, particularly since I need to stand for a good part of each day to do my job.

If you need any further information about this matter, I am sure that Dr. Holcum can provide it to you; he can be reached at 555-555-5555. Please feel free to call me if there are any questions.

Sincerely,

Randall H. Jamison

38. Letter to grocery store where customer slipped and fell:

April 16, 2003

Mr. Walter H. Gideon
Manager
Henry's Grocery Store
3111 Burt Boulevard
Calumet, Nebraska 00000

Dear Mr. Gideon:

I have been a loyal customer of Henry's since 1995.

On April 12, 2003, I made my regular weekly shopping visit to your store. When I turned into aisle three for canned and bottled goods, the floor was covered with oil. I immediately slipped and fell on the floor, and my wristwatch was smashed. Even though I was able to get up and finish my shopping, I have been quite sore for the past few days. I had to go to my doctor for a checkup after this happened, and he knows that I was quite sore and gave me instructions about what to do.

I am willing to settle this matter if you will pay me the cost of a new watch like the one that was broken ($59.95) and the cost of my doctor bill ($85.00) and things I had to buy at the drugstore for my soreness ($15.50). I think that your covering the costs of my damage is a fair way to settle this, as does my lawyer. Please let me know immediately if we can do this. Thank you.

Sincerely,

Sally R. Bridge

Enclosures

ANALYSIS

Unless you are absolutely sure that the matter is trivial and you want to settle it quickly for a small amount of money, you should consult a lawyer in any case that involves personal injury. If there is any chance whatsoever of serious or permanent injury, you should definitely consult a lawyer. Although most lawyers who handle negligence cases earn their fees by taking part of the money you receive (a "contingent fee"), a good lawyer usually makes up for this.

Ms. Bridge has thought the matter over and has made a specific demand with regard to a possible settlement. Whenever you do this, be sure that you are willing to accept what you have proposed. In many such situations, the person injured would not be agreeable to settling the matter without receiving something for pain and suffering.

Ms. Bridge should also bear in mind that everything she says or writes to anyone at Henry's Grocery Store or its insurance company can be used against her in regard to her claim.

If Ms. Bridge's own insurance company could possibly be involved, she must speak with its representative before doing anything. Making the wrong move could end Ms. Bridge's insurance coverage.

39. Letter to restaurant that served you bad food:

March 8, 2004

Mr. Gus Greasehound
Gus's Goulash and More
879 Dewdrop Lane
Clementon, New Jersey 00000

Dear Mr. Greasehound:

Last Thursday evening I took my family to your restaurant for dinner. My son ordered the chili, which was terrible, and my wife had a salad made of lettuce that looked older than she is. My daughter and I both ordered double hamburgers with all the fixings, which were delicious. Perhaps dangerous bacteria have a favorable effect on flavor: ❶ Two hours after we left the restaurant, my daughter and I were doubled over in pain and vomiting violently. We went to the emergency room at Simmons Hospital, and the doctor who treated us, Greta Winkler, M.D., diagnosed us as having serious food poisoning. We returned home to vomit the night away.

ANALYSIS

❶ There is nothing wrong with a little humor, such as Mr. Cook's remark about bacteria as seasoning, as long as you are making the point you want to make and are not being needlessly rude.

My daughter missed school the next day, and I missed work on Friday and Saturday. Neither of us was in any shape to do anything until Monday, and even then we still felt pretty bad.

We feel you owe us at least money for the terrible meals all four of us had ($76.25), my daughter's and my doctor bills at the emergency room ($50 apiece), and my two days of lost work ($165 per day). If you want to end this matter, please send me a check for the total amount ($506.25). I am enclosing copies of my receipts and my most recent pay stub to prove these expenses. If you don't want to do that, please let me know so that I may consult my lawyer about what he thinks an appropriate course of action and compensation arrangement would be. ②

Sincerely,

James M. Cook

Enclosures ③

40. Letter to County Council member regarding public works:

May 17, 2003

<u>Certified Mail</u>
<u>Return Receipt Requested</u>

Councilman John H. Adams
Fifth District
P.O. Box 905
Upperville, Kentucky 00000

Dear Mr. Adams:

I am one of your constituents, ❶ living at 1711 Thornbury Road, Upperville, Kentucky 00000. I am writing about the condition of Thornbury Road in your district.

My family and seven others live on Thornbury Road. On at least five occasions one of us has asked the Department of Public Works to repair the deep and dangerous

ANALYSIS

❶ Always advise a public official who represents you that you are his or her "constituent" and are requesting assistance because of that relationship. Public officials, especially elected ones, are very sensitive to the people they represent. It is always useful to involve other constituents, such as this letter does, if you can.

holes in the road in front of our houses. My family and the Dunster family up the street have both had damage to our cars as a result of these big holes, which have been on the road since the middle of last winter. We have had no response at all from the Department of Public Works. The condition of the road is now so bad that some people who normally use it, to make deliveries and so on, are not willing to drive on it anymore. ②

On behalf of all seven of the homeowners on this road, who are your constituents, I am requesting that you take immediate action to get the Department of Public Works to properly repair the road. We are all good taxpayers in your district and badly need your help so that the only means of getting to and from our houses will be safe for travel.

I would appreciate it if you would have someone from your office contact me as soon as you receive this letter and let me know what you will do to correct this matter. I will advise the other homeowners on the road whatever you tell me, since they are just as interested in being involved as my family is.

Sincerely,

Albert B. Finnerty

41. Letter to Internal Revenue Service regarding erroneous tax refund:

June 30, 2003

<u>Certified Mail</u>
<u>Return Receipt Requested</u>

Internal Revenue Service
P.O. Box 1000
Mystery Station, New York 10000

Re: [Your and your spouse's social
    security numbers and the tax
    year or years in question] ❶

Dear Sir or Madam:

We filed our federal income tax return for 2002 on April 8, 2003. It was filed by mail on a long form 1040. The return was prepared by a tax preparer who carefully reviewed each of our deductions and other items, and it indicated that we were entitled to a refund of $971.43. We requested that the refund be sent to us rather than be an advance payment toward this year's taxes.

On June 17, 2003, we received a refund check in the amount of $281.79 with no explanation whatsoever. We don't know whether this was an error or whether the Internal Revenue Service disagrees with something on our tax return. The tax preparer we used told us that we should have received a worksheet showing how the different refund amount was computed. We never received a worksheet. ②

On June 24, 2003, we telephoned the information service of your office and explained to Mr. Harold Greene what had occurred. Mr. Greene told us that he would review the matter and telephone us within 48 hours. We never received a telephone call from Mr. Greene.

We would appreciate it if you would provide us with the information we are seeking. If the refund of $281.79 was an error, we request that we receive the balance of our refund immediately. If the Internal Revenue Service believes that the refund we received was correct, we request that we be supplied with a worksheet so that we can review the calculations with our tax preparer. One of us can be reached at 555-555-4381 at any time if you wish to telephone us.

Thank you for your assistance.

Sincerely,

Richard E. Lee

Jennifer H. Lee ❸

❹

ANALYSIS

❸ When you write a letter to the Internal Revenue Service about a joint tax return, it is appropriate that both husband and wife sign the letter, since both have signed the joint tax return.

ANALYSIS

❹ Don't enclose additional copies of tax returns, checks, or other materials with such letters. The tax authorities have these items in their computers, and the person reviewing your letter can easily refer to them.

42. Letter to county sanitation department about poor garbage removal service:

July 19, 2003

<u>Certified Mail</u>
<u>Return Receipt Requested</u>

Mr. Ronald Michaels **❶**
Wayne County Sanitation
   Department
19200 N. Ridge Street
Wayne, New Jersey 00000

Dear Mr. Michaels:

We live at 738 Ridge Road in Wayne County, and we are supposed to have trash removed in front of our house two times a week. For a number of weeks we have not had trash collection on at least one of the two days. Last week we had trash collection on only one day, and the sanitation workers made a mess of our front lawn by upending the full garbage cans and spilling trash over our property. ❷

It disturbs me that I am not receiving the municipal services for which I pay taxes, and I want the situation corrected immediately. One of our neighbors advised me to contact County Councilman Bondsworth about this matter, but I thought it was probably best to write to you first. ❸ I would appreciate receiving a letter or a phone call from you immediately so that we will know that you are going to take appropriate steps to correct this problem.

Sincerely,

John C. Randall

43. Letter to state traffic department requesting installation of a stoplight:

September 22, 2003

Ms. Rebecca Barnes
Supervisor, Traffic Department
Utah Department of Transportation
P.O. Box 0000
Salt Lake City, Utah 00000

Dear Ms. Barnes:

My family lives at 268 Concorde Street in the Village of Pleasant View. As I am sure you know, Pleasant View has doubled in size in a little more than ten years. We are now experiencing a surge in population and, as a result, traffic. Although Concorde Street is a dead-end street at the south end, it intersects with Summit Boulevard at the north end. Summit Boulevard has become a main commuter thoroughfare now that Pleasant View is a bedroom community to the city.

The stop sign at the end of Concorde is insufficient to deal with the volume of traffic that goes down the boulevard during rush hours and many other periods of the day. We have had three accidents at that intersection in less than one year. One of them involved a cousin of mine who was visiting our house and was unable to get across the boulevard quickly enough to avoid the speeding traffic.

Everyone I know who lives on Concorde Street would like a traffic light installed at the corner of Concorde Street and Summit Boulevard. Such a light is absolutely necessary for the safety of those of us who live on Concorde Street and our visitors. It is also necessary for the safety of those who drive the boulevard every day.

I would appreciate being advised of the position of the traffic department regarding this matter. Our neighbors and I are prepared to discuss this matter with our state representatives if necessary, but we are hopeful that the traffic department already has plans to deal with it.

I look forward to hearing from you at your earliest convenience.

Sincerely,

Pamela C. Rhodes

This letter does several things that are vitally important when you make a request of a state agency. One, it provides the history of the matter that is being raised. Two, it indicates that the writer speaks for a larger group of people who have the same interest. Three, by mentioning the three accidents, this letter lets the state agency know that the writer and others are prepared to pursue the matter with their elected representatives if that is necessary.

You will virtually always receive a response to such a letter, and very often it will be highly favorable. Even if that is not the case, this kind of letter provides an excellent basis for proceeding further.

44. Letter to judge or clerk of traffic court:

If this were a case in which you were going to go to court, you could hand-deliver the letter to the judge at your hearing. Although many lawyers would disagree with me, in my experience your chances for the best possible result are probably better if you go to traffic court without a lawyer. If you hand the letter to the judge, you can explain that you wrote it before the court hearing because you want to be sure to say everything you have in mind but are very nervous.

Never challenge the integrity of a police officer in a traffic court or any other hearing. The judges in these courts see the same officers over and over again, and they almost always believe them and don't want to see their honesty challenged.

It is also a good idea never to challenge an electronic device such as a radar detector. Traffic courts obviously have to believe in the correctness of such devices and will generally feel that you are not telling the truth if you contradict them.

Ms. Wilkins's explanation in this case is a good one. She has created a basis for sympathy by telling the judge that she is a single parent caring for two children and working double shifts from time to time. It would be hard for most judges to dislike that situation.

May 15, 2003

①

Mr. Harold J. Smyth

Clerk **②**

Traffic Court of Kansas City

10000 Clark Street

Kansas City, Missouri 00000

Re: Summons No. 000000000

   Susan Wilkins

Dear Mr. Smyth:

On May 12, 2003, I received the above traffic ticket for exceeding the speed limit of 35 m.p.h. on Wilkens Avenue. According to the ticket, the radar detector determined that I was driving at a speed of 48 m.p.h. I have no argument with Officer Stanley C. Bainbridge, who issued the ticket to me, or the accuracy of the radar detector. I am guilty of speeding, and I understand that I can indicate by mail that I am pleading guilty to the charge.

The reason I am writing this letter with the summons form which I am returning is to advise the judge who will be reviewing this matter of special circumstances regarding it. In the first place, as I am sure you can verify, I have never received a moving violation ticket of any kind in the 17 years I have been driving. At

ANALYSIS

① This sort of letter need not be sent by certified mail, but should be sent in plenty of time to reach the court by the final date that is indicated. If you mail this sort of letter, be sure that the form you are to use to plead guilty is mailed with it.

ANALYSIS

② Unless you are certain which judge will be hearing your case, address this type of letter to the clerk of the traffic court, who will be responsible for giving it to the correct judge.

the time I was stopped, I was driving home from having worked a dual shift at the Ridgely Manufacturing Plant, where I am employed. The road was empty and I concede that I was rushing. I am a single mother responsible for two children, and the amount of work I must do to meet our financial needs is clearly more than I can comfortably do. I pay someone by the hour to take care of my children from the time school is over until I return home after work. The opportunity to work double shifts twice in one month and earn some extra money was very attractive to me, but the extra money I had to pay the sitter reduced the extra income by quite a lot. When I was stopped for speeding I was rushing to get home in order to avoid having to pay for an additional hour of baby-sitting. I was wrong and I know I was wrong, and my record as a driver, a mother, and a hard worker shows that I am not the kind of person who violates the law lightly.

I would greatly appreciate it if the judge who reviews this case would consider reducing the charge to a smaller one than exceeding the speed limit by more than 10 m.p.h. I would also appreciate it if he or she would consider imposing the smallest possible fine for whatever offense is appropriate. I will remit the fine promptly, whatever it is, but my tight budget will make that difficult if it is very much money.

I thank you for forwarding this letter to the appropriate judge and for your assistance in this matter.

Sincerely,

Susan Wilkins

Enclosure

45. Letter to bank that botched up checking account:

November 9, 2003

Certified Mail
Return Receipt Requested

Customer Relations Manager ❶
Industry Bank and Trust Company
521 Main Street
New York, New York 00000

Re: Checking Account No. 2873596-14

Dear Sir or Madam:

I hold checking account number 2873596-14 at your
bank and have enjoyed using it since 1994. However,
I now have a problem that I need your assistance in
solving.

On September 5, 2003, I received my normal monthly
statement. The statement was in error because it
showed that I had written a check (no. 1228) for
$1,700.49. The check was for $170.49.

On September 7, 2003, I telephoned your bank and advised the person I spoke with of this error. She said it would be corrected promptly. Unfortunately, I did not take her name. On October 6, 2003, I received my next statement for my account and it contained the same error. The next day, October 7, 2003, I was advised by a letter from your bank that two checks I had written were returned because of insufficient funds. That would not have happened if your bank had not made the error regarding the check for $170.49.

Two weeks ago I telephoned your bank and spoke with Mr. Harold Burns. I told Mr. Burns that I was demanding that the error in my statement be corrected and that I be furnished with letters of explanation and apology to Sitwell's Florist and Municipal Laundry and Dry Cleaning. These are the two checks that bounced because of your error. I also told Mr. Burns that I expected to receive credit for the fees charged for returning the two checks. This has still not been done. ②

As I am sure you can appreciate, the bank's error in this matter has caused me difficulty and embarrassment. I have done business with both the florist and the dry cleaner

ANALYSIS

② When you write such a letter, it is also important to demand everything you want to resolve the matter. Mr. Feldman is correct in asking for the letters of explanation and apology to Sitwell's Florist and Municipal Laundry and Dry Cleaning in the same letter in which he demands that his account be corrected and the fees for the returned checks be credited. Since this is a clear error on the bank's part, someone will be directed to correct it when this letter gets to the right person. You want the person who will correct the problem to know everything you demand.

for many years, and I want them to know that the mistake was yours, not mine.

Despite my repeated requests, this matter has not been corrected. Therefore, I am advising you that I will wait only another five days for you to do what you should have done immediately last month. If this matter is not corrected and the letters I have requested provided to me by that time, I will be forced to pursue appropriate legal action.

Sincerely,

Timothy H. Feldman

ANALYSIS

Note: Some banks send canceled checks or photocopies of them with customers' regular statements. If you have either form of the check, enclosing a copy with your letter should speed up the process of correcting your banking records. If you don't have your canceled checks, ask the customer relations manager to provide them.

46. Letter to bank to correct error on bank statement:

November 24, 2003

Certified Mail ❶
Return Receipt Requested

Ms. Marsha Blackburn
Customer Service Department
Friendly Savings Bank
P.O. Box 0000
St. Paul, Minnesota 00000

Re: Checking Account No. 000000000

Dear Ms. Blackburn:

I maintain checking account no. 000000000 with your bank and was a happy customer for 16 years. ❷ On my November statement I was charged for seven bounced checks. This charge was incorrect, as I had made a deposit of more than enough money more than two weeks before

ANALYSIS

❶ Ms. Summers makes her point in this letter and signals its seriousness by sending it certified mail, return receipt requested. She has used a reasonable tone in the letter, however, even though she mentions possible harm to her credit and her relationship with the bank. In most instances, a letter like this will get the attention of the bank and, hopefully, resolve the problem.

ANALYSIS

❷ Unfortunately, long relationships of relatively small depositors don't have a great deal of meaning to most banks today. Nevertheless, it is always worth mentioning that you have had a satisfactory relationship for a certain period of time and would like to continue it. Some people respect that sort of relationship, and you don't know whether your letter will be handled by one of them.

writing any of the checks that bounced. I have explained that to two people in your bank by telephone, and these charges still remain on my statement.

I would greatly appreciate your looking into this matter immediately and straightening it out. I do not want my credit or my relationship with your bank to be damaged by this matter.

Would you please let me hear from you about this at your earliest convenience? Thank you for your assistance.

Sincerely,

Meagan E. Summers

> **ANALYSIS**
> Every state regulates its banks through a state office. These offices are listed in appendix C. Even though this is a very small matter to get a state agency involved, that is always a possibility.

47. Letter to insurance salesman who has not provided a copy of insurance policy:

June 4, 2003

<u>Certified Mail</u>
<u>Return Receipt Requested</u>

Mr. Mark T. Bridge
Custom Insurance Agency, Inc.
300 N. Main Street
Austin, Texas 00000

Dear Mr. Bridge:

I have telephoned your office twice this month to request the insurance policy I purchased from you. You provided me with a summary of the policy about six weeks ago when I purchased it, but I want to have the actual policy. **1** I am sure I am entitled to receive it. I have already received my bank statement showing that the check I gave you for $382 for this year's premium was deposited a few days after I purchased the insurance policy.

I want to be absolutely sure that the insurance policy you sold me says exactly what we agreed it would say. I think I have the right to cancel this transaction if that isn't the case. If I have taken too long to make a decision whether to cancel, it is because you have not provided me with the insurance policy within a reasonable amount of time. **2**

Please send me my insurance policy within the next few days so that I can check it over. If you are unable to do so, please return my deposit and cancel the insurance.

Sincerely,

Pearl M. Lindsay

48. First letter to insurance company regarding coverage for theft:

December 28, 2003

Certified Mail **1**
Return Receipt Requested

Ms. Jane P. Fine
Claims Administrator
Underpaid Insurance Company
18907 Lone Star Highway
Dallas, Texas 00000

Re: Policy No. 000000000 **2**

Dear Ms. Fine:

ANALYSIS
1 This is the first letter to the insurance company itself and, therefore, is not threatening. It is sent by certified mail, return receipt requested, however, because the complaint concerns a lot of money and Mr. Martin wants to be sure of delivery to the appropriate person.

ANALYSIS
2 Always be certain to include your policy number in the caption of any letter you write concerning insurance.

I have had five conversations with your local office concerning the robbery of my house on October 23, 2003. Unfortunately, the robbery was a masterful job and many items of value, including cameras, paintings, jewelry, and silverware, were taken. I have provided your office with a detailed listing of the items stolen, which, as you will note, conforms to the listing in the police report. I enclose copies of the listing and the police report. I am also enclosing copies of appraisals I have received for each of the major items, which have been acquired from reputable dealers in this state. You will note that the total value of items taken comes to $47,850. **❸**

Your local representative has offered to settle this entire matter for $35,000. That is absolutely unacceptable. He says that some of the appraisals are too high, but does not specify which ones. Your company has not shown me any appraisals that differ from mine. It is clear to me that your company simply wants to pay less than I am entitled to receive according to my insurance policy.

I urge you to review this matter carefully and promptly. You may be assured that I am a reasonable person and I would like to resolve the matter with you promptly if that is at all possible. I look forward to hearing from you.

Sincerely,

William C. Martin

Enclosures

49. Second letter to insurance company regarding coverage for theft:

February 1, 2004

<u>Certified Mail</u>
<u>Return Receipt Requested</u>

Ms. Jane P. Fine
Claims Administrator
Underpaid Insurance Company
18907 Lone Star Highway
Dallas, Texas 00000

Re: Policy No. 000000000

Dear Ms. Fine:

I am greatly distressed that you have not responded to my letter of December 28, 2003, after 30 days. My house was robbed on October 23, 2003, and I have spent two months trying to get your local office, and now your headquarters, to pay my claim in accordance with my insurance policy. I feel I have made my best efforts in that regard and, accordingly, have notified Mr. Stuart Q. Friendly of the Vermont Insurance Commission of the difficulty I am having. ❶ Since Underpaid Insurance Company is an insurance company doing business in this state, I am advised by Mr. Friendly that I am entitled to have his office review the entire matter to determine whether I am being treated properly in terms of my insurance policy. I have provided Mr. Friendly with copies of all relevant materials and asked him to initiate the review process as promptly as possible. I am sure you will hear from Mr. Friendly shortly.

Sincerely,

William C. Martin

cc: Mr. Stuart Q. Friendly ❷
    Vermont Insurance
        Commission
    Department of Banking,
        Insurance and
        Securities

ANALYSIS

❶ Since he received no response to his letter trying to resolve the matter, Mr. Martin has taken the appropriate step of seeking the assistance of his state insurance commission. Insurance companies are licensed in and regulated by each state, and their continued right to do business in a state depends on a number of matters. The proper payment of bona fide claims is always important to the continued right of an insurance company to do business in a state.

ANALYSIS

❷ Once you have notified the state insurance commission of such a matter, you should be certain to copy the individual to whom you spoke there with your next letter. Mr. Martin has done that in this letter.

ANALYSIS

Note: Unless the insurance company has a good reason for not paying Mr. Martin the amount he demands, this sort of letter gives him a reasonable likelihood of receiving payment in full. Since Mr. Martin has carefully documented the value of the items stolen from his house, it does not seem the insurance company has any justified basis for refusing to pay him.

By the time you write to the main office of an insurance company or other large national business, your dealings with its local office should be concluded. The only exception to this is if you receive a call from the local office in which it is clear that the national office has told it to get the matter resolved with you.

50. Third letter to insurance company regarding coverage for theft:

February 8, 2004

<u>Certified Mail</u>
<u>Return Receipt Requested</u>

Ms. Jane P. Fine
Claims Administrator
Underpaid Insurance Company
18907 Lone Star Highway
Dallas, Texas 00000

Re: Policy No. 000000000

Dear Ms. Fine:

I have now been advised by Mr. Friendly of the Vermont Insurance Commission that the hearing in this matter will be held on April 17, 2004. I understand that you will be informed of this date by Mr. Friendly as well.

ANALYSIS

1 Once a matter is scheduled for a hearing before a state agency, you should not bargain further with your opponent. Doing so would be a sign of weakness or reluctance to attend the hearing, and that is certainly something you don't want to convey.

I am writing to advise you that I intend to have my attorney, Mary H. Powell, Esquire, at the hearing before the insurance commission. I do not feel capable of handling a matter such as this alone as a layperson. Ms. Powell advises me that she will bill me at the rate of $250 per hour for the time she spends preparing for this matter and representing me at the hearing. You are hereby notified that I intend to request that I be fully compensated for all of Ms. Powell's fees and expenses in addition to receiving full payment of my claim. ❷

Sincerely,

William C. Martin

cc: Mr. Stuart Q. Friendly ❸
    Vermont Insurance Commission,
    Department of Banking,
        Insurance and Securities
    Mary H. Powell, Esq.

ANALYSIS

❷ If there is some way you can raise the stakes a bit for the insurance company that now must prepare for the hearing, you should do so. In this case, Mr. Martin's claim to be reimbursed for the cost of an attorney he needs to represent him at the hearing is a good way of doing that. Although it is uncertain whether Mr. Martin would recover this expense even if he prevails at the hearing, there is always the possibility that he will, and the insurance company will be aware of that. In addition, the insurance company will be more concerned about the forthcoming hearing if it knows that an attorney will represent Mr. Martin.

ANALYSIS

❸ Of course, a copy of this letter should be sent to Mr. Friendly so that he will know of every communication from you once he has taken the matter under review. Your lawyer should also receive a copy of this letter, as well as all other correspondence and other related documents.

51. Letter to credit card company that has refused to correct bill:

March 19, 2003

<u>Certified Mail</u>
<u>Return Receipt Requested</u>

ABC Credit, Inc. **❶**
Attention: Customer Service
3000 Rossville Pike
Cape May, New Jersey 00000

Re: Account of Martha R. Strong
    Account No. 000000000

Dear Sir or Madam:

I have an ABC Visa card, number 000000000, and have just received my statement for February 2003. I have been asking for three months for you to give me credit for a defective lamp that was purchased at Acme Retail Furniture of Jamesboro on November 18, 2002.

ANALYSIS

❶ This is a difficult situation. Ms. Strong has apparently been unable to get the correct name of the person to whom she should send her letter. In addition, it is difficult to know what the credit card company is doing with regard to her credit and the unpaid balance. Appendix D lists the names and addresses of the main national credit companies that have information regarding the credit of millions of people. You may obtain a credit report from any of these companies by paying a small fee.

I made this request by telephone only five days after buying the lamp, and I have made it by telephone every month for the last three months. I explained in each of my telephone calls to you that the lamp is defective because it cannot possibly accommodate a standard three-way bulb without creating a serious risk of fire. My statement of February continues to show an unpaid balance that includes the price of the lamp, which was $576.80 including tax.

I returned the lamp to Acme on November 23, 2002, but for some reason neither the store nor ABC has issued me a credit. Since the lamp was defective and I brought that to your attention very promptly, I am not required to pay this amount.

I am concerned that your indifference toward this matter will damage my good credit rating, as it has damaged my confidence in your company. If my statement is not promptly corrected and if I find that my credit report has been affected, I will be forced to take appropriate legal action. **2** I hope that will not be necessary, but I feel your inaction gives me no choice.

Please let me hear from you immediately or I will assume that you do not intend to respond.

Sincerely,

Martha R. Strong

52. Letter to credit card company that botched up bill:

June 16, 2003

<u>Certified Mail</u>
<u>Return Receipt Requested</u>

Ms. Joan Loan
Customer Relations Manager
ABC Credit, Inc.
3000 Rossville Pike
Cape May, New Jersey 00000

Re: Charles H. Price ❶
    Account No. 0000-0000-0000

Dear Ms. Loan:

My last two bills from your company have been completely botched up. I telephoned your office to discuss the first bill and thought that the matter was resolved by that conversation. Now I have received a second bill containing three charges in the total amount of $1,478.32 that I did not make, and it also fails to reflect a credit for a purchase I canceled and told your office about in two different telephone calls.

> **ANALYSIS**
>
> ❶ Whenever you write to a company with which you have an account number, be certain that the caption of your letter indicates precisely the name of the account holder and the exact account number. The people who receive these letters and are responsible for handling them will bring your account up on their computers instantly with this information.

I cannot continue to do business with you on this basis. It is obviously necessary for me or any customer to receive a correct bill each month. I have done my best to straighten out this matter, but clearly have failed.

Please cancel my credit card effective today and send me a corrected final bill. I will surely have to discuss that bill with you in order to get it straight, but I am going to have to do that in any event since I must reconcile my account. I wish that it was possible to get this matter cleared up, but regrettably that does not look as if it will happen. ❷

Sincerely,

Charles H. Price

ANALYSIS

❷ Although Mr. Price is requesting that his account be closed, it is clear from the way the letter is written that he might continue to keep it open if the matter could be resolved. This is a good tactic to use in this circumstance, since the credit card company's desire is to keep as many accounts as possible. Ms. Loan might decide to instruct a member of her staff to get this matter straight no matter what it takes and keep Mr. Price's account open.

ANALYSIS

Whenever you write a letter like this, be sure that you have fully reconciled the account yourself with your receipts and other materials. Have all the necessary paperwork handy in a folder so that you can respond easily if a representative from the company should call.

53. Letter to company that failed to credit time payments:

December 15, 2003

Ms. Melissa Scott
Customer Relations Manager
Rooms and Things
34000 Sanderson Highway
Boston, Massachusetts 00000

Dear Ms. Scott:

I am in receipt of your bill dated December 3, 2003, and am writing to alert you to an error in it.

I have been paying off the furniture I bought from you last July. I started making payments this January as required by the financing agreement. I have now made 11 payments. According to the financing agreement, I am required to make 24 consecutive payments of $205.36 apiece, and then I will have paid off the whole bill. When I received my bill this month, it did not say that I had made 11 payments. It said that I had only paid $1,642.88 on my account. This comes out to 8 monthly payments instead of 11.

I have bank statements that show that I have made 11 payments to you. I am enclosing copies of those statements so that you can see them. ❶ Please straighten out my account and send me a correct bill for December. I will pay it promptly and I will make the remaining 12 payments when they are due. ❷

Sincerely,

Robin Cushion

Enclosures

54. Letter to creditor that cannot be paid promptly:

March 26, 2003

Mr. Nicholas DeLong
DeLong Custom Furniture
379 Oakwood Lane
Westport, Connecticut 00000

Re: Account No. 000000000

Dear Mr. DeLong:

I simply cannot make the payment I owe this month. I have made all my payments on time for the past 17 months, but personal hardships this month make that impossible. **1** I expect to be able to make the payment that is owed next month and am hopeful that I will then be able to continue making payments until I am paid up. I would very much appreciate it if you would let me do that, since my financial situation doesn't make anything else possible.

Please let me know if this is all right.

Thank you in advance for your consideration.

Sincerely,

Carl N. Smith

55. Letter to credit card company regarding unannounced change in interest rate:

August 24, 2003

Certified Mail
Return Receipt Requested

Customer Relations Manager
People's Credit Co.
P.O. Box 0000
Dearborn, Michigan 00000

Re: Account No. 000-000-000-000

Dear Sir or Madam:

After listening to a number of your local advertisements, I signed up for one of your credit cards. In your advertisements it was represented that the interest rate on balances under this credit card would be 9.9% and, in addition, customers would be allowed to miss one payment a year if they found it necessary.

I have used your credit card for only three months and my present balance is $13,436.79. Yesterday I received a statement indicating that the interest rate on my balance is 15.9%. That is obviously 6% higher than the interest rate I was promised when I obtained the card.

I think most people would agree that changing the interest rate that was advertised after only three months is not acceptable. Please recompute my balance using the interest rate of 9.9% that I was promised. If you intend to raise this interest rate in the future, I expect to be notified of that before the new rate is applied, so that I will have a chance to either pay off the balance or move it to another company's credit card before the rate hike.

Sincerely,

Thelma J. Lewis

ANALYSIS

This is a first-attempt letter. Ms. Lewis hopes that the credit card company will see the unfairness of changing the interest rate after only three months and restore a 9.9% interest rate for at least a reasonable period of time. Credit cards often change interest rates voluntarily to keep a customer.

If this letter fails, a subsequent, much stronger letter is appropriate.

56. Follow-up letter to credit card company regarding unannounced change in interest rate:

September 27, 2003

<u>Certified Mail</u>
<u>Return Receipt Requested</u>

Customer Relations Manager
People's Credit Co.
P.O. Box 0000
Dearborn, Michigan 00000

Re: Account No. 000-000-000-000

Dear Sir or Madam:

ANALYSIS
① Since credit card companies are large organizations, Ms. Lewis is wise to enclose a copy of her earlier letter with this one. You have no assurance that whoever receives a subsequent letter such as this will have access to your earlier correspondence.

My letter of August 24, 2003, to you (copy enclosed) ① has gone unanswered. Accordingly, I brought this matter to the attention of Mr. Freeborn Cushing of the Consumer Protection Division of the Office of the Attorney General in Santa Fe, New Mexico, and explained to him why I believe that your promised interest rate was unreasonably raised after only three months. ❷ Mr. Cushing said I could write to you again and let you know that I have brought the matter to the attention of his office and that it may be scheduled for a review conference if it is not resolved promptly. I intend to request such a conference and pursue this matter further if my interest rate is not promptly reduced to 9.9% and does not remain there for a reasonable period of time until I am notified that there will be a change.

Please send a copy of your response to this letter to Mr. Cushing at the Consumer Protection Division, Office of the Attorney General, P.O. Drawer 1508, 407 Galisteo Street, Santa Fe, New Mexico 00000. ❸

Sincerely,

Thelma J. Lewis

Enclosure

cc: Mr. Freeborn T. Cushing
   Consumer Protection Division
   Office of the Attorney General

57. Letter about problem with department store credit card:

July 22, 2003

<u>Certified Mail</u>
<u>Return Receipt Requested</u>

Customer Relations Manager
Goonies Department Store
1800 Great Northern Avenue
Milwaukee, Wisconsin 00000

Re: Account No. 0000-0000-0000

Dear Sir or Madam:

I have a Goonies credit card, number 0000-0000-0000, and use it regularly. I have been a good and satisfied customer of Goonies for 19 years. ❶

On June 25, 2003, I purchased three skirts at a clearance sale in your department store. I charged

---

ANALYSIS

❶ This letter obviously seeks to draw on the relationship Ms. Spence has with Goonies. What she is saying seems to be reasonable, and there is certainly a chance that she will succeed based on this letter.

ANALYSIS

If this approach fails, Ms. Spence can contact the division of trade and consumer protection in her state and request its assistance in the matter. Obviously Ms. Spence should have tried on all three skirts, but her reliance on the salesperson's assurance that they were all the same size is not unreasonable. Even though the legalities of this matter may be somewhat unclear, it is likely that if the state agency becomes involved, the matter will be resolved satisfactorily. It would not serve a department store's interests to be spending money and time arguing a matter like this before a state agency when it can resolve it simply by crediting Ms. Spence's account for the two skirts.

the items to my Goonies credit card in the amount of $217.50. Because I was in a rush, I tried on only one of the skirts. At the register when I hesitated about not having tried on the other two, the salesclerk assured me that all three skirts would fit the same way. I found when I got home that only the skirt I had tried on in the store fit. The two other skirts are far too small.

A couple of weeks later, at my first opportunity to do so, I came to the store and tried to return the two skirts that did not fit me. I was advised at that time that clearance sales are final and the skirts could not be returned. I explained to the woman behind the counter what had happened with regard to the skirts, but she was not sympathetic and refused the return of the skirts.

I do not think it is appropriate to rely on a technicality when a good and regular customer has been misled about a purchase in this fashion. I would appreciate it if you would arrange for me to return the two skirts and for my account to be credited in the amount of $154.87 so that I can continue to do business at Goonies and to use my credit card to do so.

Thank you for your assistance in this matter.

Sincerely,

Margaret O. Spence

58. Letter to company that is making harassing telephone calls:

February 27, 2003

<u>Certified Mail</u>
<u>Return Receipt Requested</u>

Baker Credit Collection Co.
29875 Springfield Road
Chicago, Illinois 00000

Re: Phone number 555-555-5555

Dear Sir or Madam:

ANALYSIS

1 When you complain about repeated conduct like this, it is useful to tell the other party that you are keeping a written record of it. People who become aware that someone is keeping track of what they are doing often respond to the other person because they can foresee legal consequences down the line.

For the past three months I have been receiving phone calls from solicitors working for your company. These calls are made during both the day and the evening. Each time I receive a telephone call, your solicitor will not tell me his or her last name. I get no answer when I telephone the phone number I got through the telephone company's callback service.

I have kept a written record of these phone calls for the last six weeks. **1** There have been 22 calls from your company in that time. My records show the date and time of each phone call and the first name of the solicitor. In every single conversation with your solicitors except the very first one, I requested that I not receive any further telephone calls and that my name be removed from your list. ②

If I receive one more telephone call from anyone soliciting for your company, I will take legal action. I am being harassed ③ and will not permit it to continue.

Sincerely,

Patricia A. Dougherty

ANALYSIS

② It's also important to say in such letters that you have been requesting that the solicitor stop calling you and remove your name from its records. There are legal requirements about these matters, but companies don't always observe them until they are forced to do so.

ANALYSIS

③ The use of the word "harassed" is important in these situations, since there are legal consequences to harassment and companies that solicit too heavily are aware of them. "Harassed" is a buzzword that has consequences for people in the collections business.

59. Letter to collection agency or attorney making unjustified claim:

September 15, 2003

<u>Certified Mail</u>
<u>Return Receipt Requested</u>

Quick Collection Agency
Attention: A. Smith, Collector
3500 Washington Boulevard
Birmingham, Alabama 00000

Dear Sir or Madam:

Today I received your second letter, dated September 9, demanding payment for a bed that I purchased from Drowsey's Sleep Supply on July 8, 2003. I am enclosing a copy of your letter so that you will be able to refer to it.

As I told Drowsey's Sleep Supply immediately after it was delivered, the bed is defective and I will not pay for it. The packaging is broken in several places, revealing that the mattress is cut wide open with stuffing hanging out. It looks like it was packaged by

Edward Scissorhands. I told Drowsey's that we put the bed and mattress back in the box in our garage and it can be picked up anytime.

Your two letters are improper and contain threats that you have absolutely no right to make. You have apparently not investigated the facts of this matter at all. If you had, you would know that the bed and mattress were defective and no one in her right mind would pay for them. **1** If you continue to harass me for payment that I do not owe, I will be forced to respond legally. **2** I am aware that there are laws stating what collection practices are allowed, and I intend to review this entire matter with an attorney if you make one more collection effort. **3**

I suggest that you contact your client and make arrangements for the bed and mattress to be picked up immediately.

Sincerely,

Meagan E. Martin

Enclosure

60. Letter to collection company that has been trying to collect money not owed:

August 2, 2003

Mr. James L. Brown
Manager of Operations
Intercontinental Credit Collection Company
P.O. Box 23665
Atlanta, Georgia 00000

Dear Mr. Brown:

For the past four weeks my husband and I have received several telephone calls a week pressing us for payment of a bill from George's Upholstery Company for reupholstering our sofa and two chairs. We advised this company when they delivered our furniture that we did not have the slightest intention of paying for the work. Our furniture was re-covered in the wrong fabric, and if that weren't bad enough, the workmanship was shoddy. We will have to have the job redone by a company that honors its customers' wishes and prides itself on good craftsmanship.

Your constant telephone calls and the letters you have written are harassing ① us beyond the limit of any reasonable collection efforts. Now that you know that we are not going to pay this bill for the reasons I have explained, ② we expect all of these efforts to stop immediately. We understand that both federal and state laws place serious restrictions on the collections efforts that are allowed. ③ If your contacts with us do not stop immediately, we will review this matter with an attorney and determine what further steps are appropriate. ④

Sincerely,

Paula S. Graham

61. Letter to someone who owes money for work:

This is a very unpleasant situation. Mr. and Mrs. Wright are watching Ms. Culpepper work in their house and trying to avoid paying her. Ms. Culpepper wants to finish the job, but she also wants to get paid immediately for the work she has done.

June 4, 2003

Mr. and Mrs. Jonathan W. Wright
1000 Apple Street
Orange Grove, Virginia 00000

Dear Mr. and Mrs. Wright:

I was hired by you on May 27, 2003, to clean out your basement, scrub the floor and walls, and white-wash the walls with paint you selected. We agreed that I would charge $12 an hour for my work and the job would take approximately six work days. I told you that I needed to be paid every two days to keep up with my expenses and you agreed to do that.

I worked on May 29 and 30, 2003, and I left a note at your house requesting payment for 9½ hours of work. This comes to $114 at the $12 per hour rate we agreed upon.

Although you didn't pay the bill I left you for the first two days, I worked another 13 hours on May 31 and June 2, 2003. When I saw you in the middle of the day on June 2, I reminded you that I was supposed to be paid. You told me I would be paid when you returned from the bank in about an hour, but when you came back to the house you said that you forgot to get my money. I left at about 2:15 p.m. that afternoon. **1**

I have now not been paid for 22½ hours of work, which comes to $270. I need to be paid immediately, as we agreed, so that I can pay my own expenses.

I want to finish the job to your satisfaction, and I will do that as soon as I am assured that I will be paid for my work. I gather that you are very busy, so I will be happy to stop by again to pick up the payment. Please let me know when that would be convenient. **2**

Sincerely,

Brandy T. Culpepper

ANALYSIS

1 By stating exactly what happened on each date and precisely how much money they owe her, Ms. Culpepper is demonstrating that she is prepared for further action if that is needed. It is not necessary for her to make an express threat to use that information in this letter, since Mr. and Mrs. Wright will surely get the point.

ANALYSIS

2 Ms. Culpepper could have stopped working when she didn't get paid as agreed for the first two days, but she was probably hoping she'd get paid. For diplomatic reasons Ms. Culpepper has not stated that she will not work further until she is paid, but anyone reading this letter would assume that is likely. This letter allows Mr. and Mrs. Wright to pay Ms. Culpepper and let her finish the job without losing face.

62. Letter to friend or relative who owes money:

August 24, 2003

Mr. John Baxter
306 Townsend Avenue
Bridgeport, Connecticut 00000

Dear John:

I am very sorry to have to write this letter.

When I loaned you $4,000 in March, I was trying to help you out of the very difficult situation you told me you were facing. I was happy to do it provided you paid me back within two months, as you promised. It has now been five months since I loaned you the money, and I have had to ask you many times to repay me.

I am in a real bind here. I need that money very badly, but I hate the thought of doing anything legal to get it. I thought that if I wrote a letter you would understand how serious this matter is for me and pay me back immediately. I really hope you will, because I want to continue the good relationship we had before this matter came up.

Please call me and let me know
what you are going
to do.

Yours,

Frank

A letter to a friend or relative should obviously not be sent by certified mail.

The tone of this letter is clearly different from the tone of a letter to a businessperson. This sort of letter does not specifically threaten legal action, but makes it clear that Frank wants to get his money back.

It's useful in this kind of letter to ask for a specific response, as Frank has done. The hope with this kind of letter is that the friend or relative will realize how serious you are and pay you back.

Another strategy in a letter like this is to lay off the heaviness on someone else. For example, you can tell a friend that your lawyer or accountant or business partner or some other third party is insisting that you do something to get your money back. This is a little like the car dealer who becomes your friend and ally against the manager in the back, whom you never see.

63. Letter to neighbor regarding property line dispute:

This letter is obviously written in a very different tone from one being sent to a stranger. When the personal relationship between you and someone like a neighbor is important, you can always get your point across without threats or harsh language.

June 21, 2003

1

Dear Bob:

ANALYSIS

1 Note that there is no address line on this letter. A first letter to your next-door neighbor should not need one, as presumably you are on cordial terms with the people living there and you can drop the letter in their box yourself.

I really wish that we weren't having a problem about the property line.

As I told you, I am sure that the place where you put your new storage shed is over the property line between our houses. We wouldn't care about this very much if it were temporary, but as it looks like the shed is going to be a permanent fixture, it should be on your property. I know you feel strongly that the shed is on your property, and the only way I can think of to solve the problem is to ask a surveyor to check it out.

I asked Elmer Hargrove if he would take a look sometime when he had work in the neighborhood. Elmer is doing a survey for a swimming pool right around the corner, and he told me he will check out the property line next week. ② I wanted you to know in case you see someone walking around the property and checking it. I will let you know as soon as Elmer has looked things over, and of course, you can call me about it anytime.

Best wishes,

Michelle

64. Letter to offensive neighbor:

October 17, 2003

Mr. and Mrs. Scott J. Stevens
9023 Pine Ridge Road
Mobile, Alabama 00000

Dear Mr. and Mrs. Stevens:

I wish I didn't have to write this letter, but the noise from your children's stereo is unbearable at our house. We were unable to go to sleep until 2:00 A.M. twice last week. The noise from the stereo and the loud voices of the young people at parties on both Friday and Saturday nights kept us awake until that time.

This problem has been going on for four months. My husband and I have honestly tried our best to explain it to you and find a way to get it stopped. Nothing we have said seems to have made any difference, and we are now at the point where we can't continue to live in our house. As you know, my husband has not been well the past few years, and it is very important that he get enough sleep at night. ① When he went to see his doctor last week, the doctor noticed his condition and asked him about how much sleep he was getting. When the doctor heard what was going on, he told us that my husband's health is being damaged by staying awake and if it continues he may wind up in the hospital. ②

Please do something immediately to stop the noise from occurring.

Sincerely,

Susan P. Stone

ANALYSIS

② Whenever possible, something involving another person's statements or advice is useful in such matters. In this case, Mrs. Stone's letter tells her neighbors what her husband's doctor has said. This is a good approach because any reasonable person would understand from that information that the Stones have no choice if the noise does not stop. When the advice comes from someone like a doctor, it takes the personal aspect out of the dispute.

ANALYSIS

Although Mrs. Stone's letter does not threaten legal action, it is clear that legal action may be necessary if the problem is not solved. You don't want to state the possibility of legal action outright in letters to friends, relatives, or neighbors.

Letters to friends, relatives, or neighbors should not be certified. You want a letter like this to sound serious but not official or standoffish. This one, unlike the others, does include the neighbor's address because its tone is more formal and because the Stevenses may not be the family right next door.

65. Letter to principal of public school attended by child with problem:

December 18, 2003

Certified Mail ①
Return Receipt Requested

Mrs. Joyce L. Quincy
Principal ②
Public School No. 123
87 Palm Drive
Miami, Florida 00000

Dear Mrs. Quincy:

I am the mother of Judy Applegate, a student in the fourth grade at PS 123. Judy has been at your school since first grade; she has done well in her studies and has never had any behavior problems. You may be aware that Judy is a little small for her age.

All of this school year and most of last year, Judy has been teased about her size by some of the boys in her class. At first she tried to avoid the boys who are teasing her, but that has proved to be impossible. The teasing has reached the point now where it happens in class when the teacher is not looking and also during recesses and gym periods. Judy has come home on several occasions depressed and crying because of these experiences.

I have spoken with several of Judy's teachers about the matter, but it has not helped. Last month my husband and I attended a conference with Judy's homeroom teacher, Mrs. Leona Haverford, and we explained everything to her. Mrs. Haverford said she would do her best to put a stop to the problem, but that has not happened.

My husband and I believe it is time for you as the principal of the school to intervene. Our daughter is not receiving the education she is entitled ❸ to under these circumstances. We feel it is the obligation of PS 123 to make it possible for

Judy to attend school comfortably, and that is certainly not happening.

I would appreciate hearing from you regarding this matter as promptly as possible.

Sincerely,

Victoria M. Applegate ④

ANALYSIS

④ Mrs. Applegate has chosen not to send copies of this letter to Mrs. Leona Haverford, Judy's homeroom teacher. This is probably a good choice, since Mrs. Haverford, if she received a copy, would probably spend more time defending herself to Mrs. Quincy than stopping the problem. A school principal such as Mrs. Quincy has probably dealt with this sort of problem in other instances and has the authority to tell Mrs. Haverford what to do about it.

66. Letter to superintendent of schools after unsatisfactory response from school principal:

January 4, 2004

<u>Certified Mail</u> 1
<u>Return Receipt Requested</u>

ANALYSIS

1 This letter should definitely be sent by certified mail, return receipt requested, since the Applegates have now struck out with Judy's homeroom teacher and the principal.

Mr. Robert F. Rutherford
Superintendent of Schools
Florida Department of Education
340 Orange Lane
Miami, Florida 00000

Dear Mr. Rutherford:

My daughter, Judy, is a fourth-grade student at PS 123.

During most of Judy's third-grade year and all of her fourth-grade year so far, she has been subjected to serious and hurtful teasing by some of the boys in her class. Judy is a little small for her age, and these boys apparently find that a reason to pick on her. The actions of these boys have become intolerable to Judy and are affecting her schoolwork.

ANALYSIS

② Since the Applegates are now going above the principal's head, it is important to let the superintendent know that they tried Mrs. Quincy first. The best way to do this is to enclose a copy of Mrs. Applegate's letter to Mrs. Quincy, as they have done. You should do this whenever you write to someone's superior, because you want to let that person know that you gave the lower official a fair chance to solve the problem.

My husband and I have had several conversations about this with Judy's teachers, but it did not help. On December 18, 2003, I wrote a letter about it to the principal, Mrs. Joyce L. Quincy. ② I am enclosing a copy of that letter so that you will be aware of what I told Mrs. Quincy. Even after that letter, to which I never got a response, the problem has continued.

We believe that as Superintendent of Schools you have the responsibility for dealing with this matter in a way that makes it possible for our daughter to continue to attend her school in a comfortable way. We would appreciate it if you would advise us as promptly as possible what action you will take. I am sure you can appreciate how concerned my husband and I are

about the welfare of our daughter at
her school.

Sincerely,

Victoria M. Applegate

Enclosure ③

ANALYSIS

③ Enclosing the letter
to Mrs. Quincy is also
useful because the Apple-
gates can then be certain
that Mr. Rutherford has
received exactly the same
information as Mrs. Quincy
received. Higher officials
such as superintendents
generally deal with matters
like this by letting the lower
official know they want
the problem solved. Mrs.
Applegate has given
Mr. Rutherford enough
information for this pur-
pose by giving him a copy
of her letter to Mrs. Quincy.

67. Letter to county school board regarding negligent school bus driver:

January 10, 2003

<u>Certified Mail</u>
<u>Return Receipt Requested</u>

Chase County School Board
101 Winters Lane
Chase, Kentucky 00000

Dear Members of the School Board:

I am writing to advise you that the morning driver of county school bus number 19 is grossly negligent. ❶

My husband and I live on Sunset Avenue, which as you surely know is a very busy street. Our two children, ages 11 and 13, are picked up by school bus 19 on Sunset Avenue in the morning between 7:30 and

7:45 A.M. ② The bus passes right in front of our house.

The person driving this school bus is endangering the children. The driver is not pulling the bus all the way over to the right before opening the door, and she is closing the door and driving away too quickly after children get off the bus. Sunset Avenue is quite wide, and the children don't have enough time to cross the street before the school bus starts to drive away—which is a signal to cars on both sides of the street to proceed. We have seen this happen on many occasions and specifically watched it happen three times last week. On one occasion we witnessed a speeding car that barely missed hitting a child who had not made it to the curb by the time traffic began moving. We fear for our children's safety in the hands of this apparently impatient, careless driver.

We know that the school bus system is your responsibility, and my husband and I ask you to look into this matter immediately.

Sincerely,

Frances L. Short

68. Letter to school principal requesting special accommodation for child:

Whenever you request an accommodation from a large institution or a state agency, be certain to explain fully why it is needed.

September 6, 2002

Mr. Jonathan C. Smart
Principal
Clifton Elementary School
1000 Education Lane
Clifton Park, Mississippi 00000

Dear Mr. Smart:

Our daughter, Samantha, is in the fourth grade at Clifton Elementary School. Samantha is experiencing very bad allergies to pollen in the fall and spring seasons. On most days it is difficult for her to attend gym classes in the outdoor yard. Her allergies get so bad that she is almost unable to breathe. She is being treated by Dr. Henry J. Peterson at County Medical Center, and we hope that her health will improve in the near future.

We are requesting that Samantha be excused from attending outdoor gym classes during the fall and spring seasons, when her allergies are worst. Samantha's difficulties do not seem to be too great inside the gym, and she could certainly participate in her gym classes there instead of in the yard at these times. **1**

I will get Dr. Peterson to write a letter to you if you would like to have one about this matter. **2** Please let me know as soon as possible if this accommodation could be made for our daughter. **3**

Thank you.

Sincerely,

Alvin P. Potter

69. Letter to landlord who has not returned security deposit:

June 4, 2003

Certified Mail
Return Receipt Requested

Mr. Joseph C. Burns
Crossroads Apartments
521 Linthicum Lane
Bridgeport, Connecticut 00000

Dear Mr. Burns:

I moved out of my apartment in your building on April 30, 2003, and you still have not returned my security deposit. I spoke with your agent about this on May 5, 2003, and with a woman named Colleen in your office on May 13, 2003. It has now been over a month since I moved out of the apartment, and you know that no damage whatsoever was done to the apartment.

You have violated the terms of the lease, which reads "the balance of said security deposit shall be returned to tenant in full, together with interest, upon expiration of the term of this Lease and vacation of the apartment." ❶ I do not intend to wait longer than one week from today to receive this money. If I do not get it, I will take appropriate legal action. ❷

Sincerely,

Rachel L. Johnson

70. Letter to office building that is not wheelchair accessible:

May 5, 2003

Certified Mail
Return Receipt Requested

Mr. Chester C. Vorhees
Manager
The Seafield Building
2050 Seafield Boulevard
Philadelphia, Pennsylvania 00000

Dear Mr. Vorhees:

I understand that you are the manager of the office building located at 2050 Seafield Boulevard in Philadelphia.

I am confined to a wheelchair. My accountant is on the ninth floor of your office building, and I need to visit him a few times a year to do my taxes and other things. Regrettably, your building is not accessible to people in wheelchairs. **1**

There is a four-inch step between the parking area in the basement of the building and the floor where the elevator is located, and there is no ramp. This is very difficult and dangerous for people like me. In addition, there are no wheelchair-accessible bathrooms on the ninth floor of the building, where my accountant has his offices. On two occasions I have been forced to go to the tenth floor to use the bathroom. This is inconvenient and embarrassing. ❷

I would very much appreciate your taking immediate steps to make your office building fully wheelchair accessible so that I may continue to do business there. Would you please advise me by return mail what you propose to do about this problem?

Thank you in advance for your consideration.

Sincerely,

Roger T. Phelps

71. Letter to employer regarding sexual harassment:

There are two basic kinds of sexual harassment. There is what is known as "quid pro quo" sexual harassment, which occurs when someone offers an employee a specific work-related benefit, or threatens a specific work-related harm, if the employee does not engage in some kind of sexual activity. The other kind of sexual harassment is known as "sexually charged workplace" harassment. This is sexual harassment in which a specific proposition to an employee is not made, but the amount of sexual talk, gestures, or suggestions is offensive to an employee and disruptive to her or his work.

Sexual harassment is absolutely prohibited by federal and state laws. Anyone who believes she or he is being sexually harassed at the workplace should take immediate clear action demanding that it be stopped. No employer in his right mind today would ignore a complaint about sexual harassment.

Most employee handbooks discuss this subject and tell employees what to do if they experience sexual harassment. You should follow the directions in your employee handbook if they are reasonable and workable. If not, you should do whatever you need to do to get the full attention of someone who has the authority to stop the matter.

March 26, 2003

<u>Certified Mail</u>
<u>Return Receipt Requested</u>

Mr. Arnold C. Butterworth ❶
Director of Human Relations
ABC Widget Manufacturing
    Company
7782 Astoria Boulevard
New Forest, Delaware 00000

Dear Mr. Butterworth:

I am writing to confirm a serious
matter that I discussed with you
yesterday.

ANALYSIS

❶ Ms. Dougherty has wisely taken time to identify the correct person in her company to speak to and write to about this matter. You should certainly do that in any instance this serious, so that immediate action can be taken to end the offensive conduct. No employee should tolerate sexual harassment. In most instances, a letter like this will end the matter. If it does not, you should immediately contact either the state or federal agencies that are available at all times to help you with this problem.

I have been employed by ABC Widget Manufacturing
Company for seven years, and I have received three
promotions during that time. I currently serve as
assistant quality control reviewer. My department consists of 27 men and 4 women; my immediate supervisor and his supervisor are both men.

Since I joined the company in 1996, I have been exposed
to a considerable amount of discussion regarding sexual
matters during my workday. I have been reluctant to
speak out about this matter because only two women in
our department are exposed to it regularly and I do not

want us to have bad relations with the men. I am sure you can appreciate that it is difficult to criticize other workers, especially superiors, for their conversations.

In recent weeks, the sexual discussions between some of the men in this department have increased. In addition, the men are using vulgar language and making obscene gestures. I find it very difficult to keep my mind on my work while this occurs, and it makes me terribly uncomfortable. When I discussed the matter with my husband, he advised me to write this letter to you.

I want this situation ended immediately so that I can do my job comfortably without being embarrassed and distracted by it. I know that I may pursue this matter with state or federal agencies if I choose to do so, but obviously that would be very unpleasant for all involved.

I would appreciate it if you would let me know as promptly as possible what action you intend to take. And I thank you in advance for keeping my name confidential as you investigate the matter.

Sincerely,

Stella R. Dougherty

72. Letter to co-worker about sexual harassment:

Although no employee should ever accept sexually unwelcome conduct at the workplace, it is important to bear in mind that people are sometimes mistaken about what conduct is acceptable to another person. Obviously overt physical conduct of a sexual nature at the workplace is never acceptable. But a fair and reasonable person can occasionally be mistaken about whether humorous remarks or even an overture toward dating will be acceptable to someone else. When you find such remarks unacceptable, make yourself perfectly clear without being harsh or rude. If that does not work, a personal letter like this is a reasonable next step. If that fails, the involvement of a third party is absolutely necessary. In businesses of all sizes, today's employee handbooks generally cover the subject of sexual misconduct and advise employees how to proceed should it occur.

May 5, 2004

<u>Personal</u>
<u>Hand Delivered</u>

Ms. Rebecca Black ❶
The Waterford Agency
305 Holt Lane
Annapolis, Maryland 00000

Dear Ms. Black:

I am writing this personal letter to advise you confidentially of conduct you are engaging in with me that is not acceptable. I write in the hope that you will understand and respect my discomfort regarding what you are doing and stop it immediately. I would prefer, and assume you would also, to resolve this matter privately.

When you enter my office while no one else is there, as you do frequently in the course of our work, you assume poses and come into physical contact with me in ways that make me very uncomfortable. Sometimes you come so close to me that I am afraid there will be unwelcome physical contact. As I am sure you can see, I am a very reserved person and I want others to respect my privacy. It is my preference that no interaction of a sexual or flirtatious nature whatsoever take place where I work.

In addition, you have on at least three occasions made risqué and sexually forward comments to me. I do not know precisely what you intend by those comments, but they make me uncomfortable and I want them to stop. ②

I hope and trust that this letter will end these difficulties once and for all so that we can have a cordial professional relationship.

Sincerely,

Joshua Moon

73. Letter to employer requesting promotion:

November 7, 2002

<u>Hand Delivered</u> **1**

AN ALYSIS

1 For obvious reasons, this letter should not be sent by mail but hand delivered instead.

Seymour L. Barron, M.D.
Vice President, Medical Affairs
Gernsey Hospital
2000 Ourtime Boulevard
Louisville, Kentucky 00000

Dear Dr. Barron:

As you know, I am completing my three-year contract as a member of the Neurology Department of the hospital. I have been very satisfied with my work at Gernsey and the Chief of Neurology, Dr. Cannon, has praised my work on numerous occasions. Other than increases in my salary due to larger numbers of patients being treated, I have received no raises during the three-year period. **2**

AN ALYSIS

2 A letter seeking a promotion or raise of any kind should always review, very briefly, the employee's record of job performance. It should also always mention people such as supervisors who will provide favorable opinions about the employee's work. Although you can assume that the people in charge of these matters have access to your full employment records, it doesn't hurt to refer to them when they contain favorable things.

I understand that the position of Assistant Chief of the Department of Neurology is now available. I feel certain that Dr. Cannon will recommend me for that position, and I would like to be seriously considered for it. I have the training and experience necessary for the position. I have told Dr. Cannon that I intend to advise you of my interest in the position, and she has been very encouraging.

Please let me know at your convenience what further steps I might take to supply you and the committee with whatever information you need about me. I have enjoyed my work at Gernsey these past three years and look forward to continuing in the service of this hospital. ❸

Sincerely,

Patrick K. Johnson

ANALYSIS

❸ Since every employer is interested in employees who continue to work for it for substantial periods of time, anyone seeking a raise or promotion is well advised to indicate that he is happy with his employment and looks forward to continuing.

74. Letter to travel agent who misled people about a trip:

August 8, 2002

<u>Certified Mail</u>
<u>Return Receipt Requested</u>

Ms. Rebecca Blake
Worldwide Travel Agency
721 Alameda Avenue
Richmond, California 00000

Dear Ms. Blake:

I am writing to express my great unhappiness regarding the trip to Mexico you sold my husband and me. We have just returned from that trip, and we are most unhappy about the additional expenses we incurred.

We learned of this trip from several local newspaper advertisements placed by your company. Those advertisements stated that the total price of $1,250 per person, double occupancy, was "all inclusive." Those words mean that we would have no further expenses if we bought the packages. You confirmed that this was the case when we spoke with you on July 11, 2002.

We found when we took the trip that we had to pay additional expenses, including local transportation from the airport to and from the hotel, fees for some of the water activities, and fees for meals on the boat trip that was advertised as part of the package. The cost for these additional items came to $230 apiece, for a total of $460. I enclose our receipts. ❶

We bought this trip because it looked like a good deal. We are on a very tight budget, and we have now spent more money than we had available for this purpose. We believe that this is due to your misleading advertisements and the misleading advice you gave us. ❷ I am writing to demand that you refund the $460 that we were required to spend during this trip. If that does not occur, my husband and I will pursue appropriate legal action.

Sincerely,

Pamela C. Rivers

Enclosures

ANALYSIS

❶ Obviously there are some people who assume that there will be extras when they buy a travel package and others, on tight budgets, who assume that nearly everything will be covered. Mr. and Mrs. Rivers fall into the latter group, and they were not prepared to spend any additional money on this trip.

ANALYSIS

❷ The suggestion that there has been a misrepresentation raises serious legal concerns in many situations. This is especially so when there has been advertising and also when something occurs in interstate commerce. By saying that she and her husband have been "misled," Mrs. Rivers is making absolutely clear to Worldwide Travel Agency that there was a misrepresentation to them.

Unfortunately the travel industry has had more than a few claims regarding trips that were either substantially different from those that were advertised or trips that were not provided at all. It pays to deal with a reputable travel agent in these matters, since it is often difficult to determine precisely who is financially responsible if a trip does not turn out as planned.

75. Letter to hotel regarding bad services:

April 20, 2003

Ms. Susan Blake
Manager
Oakshire Hotel
2000 Main Street
Boise, Idaho 00000

Dear Ms. Blake:

My husband and I stayed at your hotel for one night on April 16, 2003. Three items in our room, the television, the hot water faucet, and the coffee heater, were broken when we arrived, and were not fixed until four hours into our stay. Then during the night the pipes in the bathroom began groaning and dripping so loudly that we had to stop the noise by putting towels under the leak. We lost a good deal of sleep as a result of this. To make matters worse, your desk clerk forgot to deliver to my husband an urgent fax that had arrived overnight, and, as a result, my husband's business plans were ruined.

We provided our credit card number to your hotel when we checked in, and I am sure that the room charges were placed on it. Because we had to move to another hotel and were extremely rushed, we did not have time to argue with the desk clerk about the matter or to call the credit card company to dispute the charge. We paid $165 for our room in your hotel. For that price, we were entitled to much better accommodations and much better treatment.

We have advised our credit card company that this charge should not be processed or paid. I am writing to advise you that we are doing that and to request that you cancel the charge. ① We understand that there is a formal procedure available if you refuse to do this and we will follow that procedure if necessary. ② In all honesty I do not see how you could possibly charge us for the miserable service you rendered.

Please advise me in writing of your intentions.

Sincerely,

Sarah L. Conner

76. Letter to hotel that did not honor reservation:

July 10, 2003

Mr. Mark J. Weinstein
Manager
Sunrise Hotel
25090 Sunset Strip
St. Louis, Missouri 00000

Dear Mr. Weinstein:

On July 3, 2003, through your 800 telephone number, I booked a reservation for two nights, July 8 and 9, 2003, in your hotel. When I arrived on July 8, I was told by the desk clerk that although my reservation was on file, I could not be provided with a room because of overbooking. It was about 7:30 p.m. by the time I arrived, and I was exhausted from traveling for almost 14 hours from London. I had business meetings beginning at 8:30 the next morning in St. Louis and had planned to eat a very light dinner in my hotel room and retire early. The desk clerk proceeded to telephone other hotels in the vicinity and, after approximately one and a half hours, found a room for me at the Slovenly Arms

Hotel three blocks from yours. Not only did this incident cause me considerable aggravation, not to mention a most unpleasant three-block walk in St. Louis in the nighttime with two large suitcases, but the room I was provided at the Slovenly Arms would certainly explain the abysmal reputation of that hotel. Your error resulted in no small amount of personal discomfort and great difficulty concentrating at my business meetings the next morning.

I will be in St. Louis once again approximately three weeks from now. Given what occurred last time, I would hope that you would provide me with a room for two evenings gratis. Your hotel is used regularly by several people in my company, Colossal Finishers, which maintains a regional office in St. Louis. I am sure you wish to retain the favorable business that I and my colleagues provide to you. ①

ANALYSIS

① This is a situation in which, unfortunately, considerable inconvenience has been experienced but there is really no sound legal basis for a claim. On the other hand, hotels are among the businesses in which public relations are terribly important. Ms. Fox has explained to the manager that her company uses the hotel on a regular basis. When you write a letter like this, there is a reasonable chance that you will receive a favorable response. Some hotels give free or reduced-price accommodations or meals in their restaurants to customers who have been inconvenienced.

ANALYSIS

If the hotel or motel that has inconvenienced you is part of a national or international chain, and the local hotel or motel does not respond appropriately, you may receive satisfaction by writing to the national office. National hotel and motel chains are conscious of their general reputation and will often lean on an individual establishment to perform in a certain way to keep their overall reputation intact.

I would like to receive confirmation by fax that a room has been reserved for me for the evenings of August 3 and 4, 2003. My fax number is on this letterhead.

Sincerely,

Bernadette A. Fox

77. Letter to airline regarding additional cost of later flight:

April 2, 2003

Certified Mail
Return Receipt Requested

Mr. John L. Ethridge
Customer Relations Manager
Sky Runner Airlines, Inc.
Sky Runner Building
Albuquerque, New Mexico 00000

Dear Mr. Ethridge:

I have enjoyed flying with Sky Runner Airlines for many years and have never had anything but pleasant experiences with your firm. That changed last month when your poor service cost me time, money, and peace of mind.

On March 8, 2003, I arrived two and a half hours early for my flight number 2692 from John F. Kennedy Airport in New York to Los Angeles International Airport. I had purchased my ticket from your office in Bronx, New York, two weeks prior to that date. Upon arrival I was advised that the flight had been canceled and no substitute flight was offered by your airline. No one from Sky Runner offered me any help in making contingency plans. On our own, some of the other passengers and I ultimately managed to secure seats on the scheduled flight of Padonia Airways that departed at the same time. Padonia Airways charged me an additional $216.50 for the replacement flight. ① Although I understand that you are required by law to pay for my transportation after you canceled my flight, I was unable to sort out the details before the Padonia Airlines flight left, so I paid the $216.50 and boarded the flight. I am enclosing copies of my Sky Runner ticket and the ticket I purchased from Padonia Airlines. I expect to be reimbursed.

When I telephoned your office in New York to arrange reimbursement, I was told that the staff of that office could not help me. I have made numerous phone calls to your offices and never been clearly told who is

responsible for correcting this situation. Since you are
the manager of customer relations, I am writing
to you, and this is the last communication I intend
to have with your airline regarding the matter. If I
do not receive a refund of the $216.50 promptly,
I will take appropriate steps to recover the money,
which I am clearly owed.

Sincerely,

John E. Carmichael

78. Letter to airline customer relations manager regarding overbooked flight:

June 21, 2003

Mr. Charles Wings
Customer Relations Manager
Ambassador Airlines
P.O. Box 1234
Boise, Idaho 00000

Dear Mr. Wings:

I bought an e-ticket two weeks in advance for your
Perdunk-to-Seatuck flight on June 7, 2003. When
I arrived at the airport—two and half hours ahead of
time—I went straight to the gate as I had been told
to do when I purchased the ticket. I tried to check
in right away but was told that I had to wait. So
I waited. Then it became clear that a different flight
had been canceled and that those passengers were
being rebooked on my flight. I became concerned, so
I tried to check in again. Again, I was told to take a
seat and wait; they weren't ready for me yet.

When I was finally told that I could check in, the member of your staff I was dealing with informed me that the flight was full and that I would not get on the plane. I told him that I had been waiting for two hours, not allowed to check in, and that I had a ticket. He told me that although I had a ticket, I did not have a seat. You only get a seat when you check in. (Was it unclear when I purchased my ticket that I wanted a seat on the airplane?)

Needless to say, I was incensed, so I asked to see your manager. By the time she arrived, the gates were locked and the plane was leaving the boarding area. Your manager made arrangements for me to have a seat on a flight from Perdunk to Seatuck leaving three hours later. I had no choice but to take that flight, so I was an hour and a half late for a very important meeting. As you can see, I suffered considerable inconvenience as a result of not being allowed onto the flight for which I had purchased a ticket.

I'd rather not get into an argument about what an airline must do when it has booked you on a flight and there is no seat. As your records will show, I am a regular user of your airline and many colleagues at my business are as well. I deserved better treatment than I received from you on this occasion, and I believe I should be compensated for what occurred. The fair compensation under these circumstances would be the refund of my airfare one-way from

Perdunk to Seatuck, which is $138.
I do not want to make a federal case
out of this matter, and hope that you
will respond favorably to this request
so that I will want to fly Ambassador
again. **(1)**

Sincerely,

Jacqueline Daniels

ANALYSIS

(1) Although various rules apply to airlines when they don't seat you on scheduled flights, they are complex. There are also situations in which airlines are forced at the last minute to provide seats to certain passengers. You can spend your whole life trying to figure out what occurred in your situation and what the airline is required to do or does as a matter of its own policy in such circumstances. The best way to present this matter is to tell the airline what happened and why you are requesting that something be done about it. The airline may respond favorably to you because the law requires it, and it may respond favorably to you because you are valued as a customer. Either way you'll have satisfaction.

79. Letter to government official who is threatening action against you:

April 16, 2003

<u>Certified Mail</u>
<u>Return Receipt Requested</u>

Tax Collection Agency
Franklin P. Hart, Auditor
P.O. Box 0000
Wichita, Kansas 00000

Re: Johnson Grocery Store
     12-1234567

Dear Mr. Hart:

In your letter of February 18, 2003, and in three telephone calls thereafter, you advised me that the state authorities do not feel I have paid the correct amount of retail sales tax for my business. I have checked that matter very carefully and assure you that I have. In both of my

> **ANALYSIS**
> **1** When a government agency or official is unjustifiably making your life difficult, you should be certain to fully explain your position in writing.

stores there are continuous tape cash registers that record every single sale. The retail sales taxes I have paid have been exactly what I owe based on those tapes, and they are available to you if you wish to review them. **1**

Your constant threats of an audit if I do not agree to an acceptable compromise are absolutely improper. I do not owe any money for these taxes, and there is no reason for me to compromise. Given that I am in the right, I can assure you that an audit would certainly be more welcome to me than your inappropriate threats.

I have contacted the office of my state representative, Mr. Henry C. Stanhope, and scheduled an appointment for next week. I told Mr. Stanhope's assistant that the matter I want to discuss concerns retail sales taxes. If you would like to be present at that meeting to express your views and answer questions, please feel free to come. The meeting will be at Mr. Stanhope's office in the Municipal Building on Cason Street at 1:00 p.m. on April 21, 2003. **2**

Sincerely,

Robert T. Johnson

ANALYSIS

2 If you can do so without threatening, it is often useful to put the government official on the spot. Mr. Johnson did that by inviting Mr. Hart to a meeting with his state representative. He also did it by indicating that an audit would be perfectly satisfactory to him.

Unfortunately some government officials do not restrain themselves in proper ways and sometimes try to achieve results to which the government is not entitled. As long as you have a good explanation for your actions, don't be shy about telling the government official what you believe.

80. Letter to someone threatening to sue you:

November 7, 2003

Certified Mail
Return Receipt Requested

Mr. James T. Stanley
407 Forest View Road
Shipley Heights, Texas 00000

Dear Jim:

I have received your letter threatening to sue me for not repairing work that I did in your master bathroom. What you are claiming is totally unjustified. ❶ If you file a lawsuit, that will be an act of malice with no reasonable basis. ❷

I completed work in your bathroom about six weeks ago. One of the items you ordered, custom-made glass doors for the shower, was not installed at that time because of a delivery delay. Our understanding was that you would use a shower curtain until the doors were completed

ANALYSIS

❶ When someone is threatening to sue you for something that is not your fault, the most useful thing you can do is fully explain the matter in a letter such as this and tell the other person that the suit would be malicious and groundless (or baseless).

ANALYSIS

❷ A letter like this places you in the best possible position if the other party does file a suit against you. It also provides the greatest chance that you will not be sued, particularly if the other party has a lawyer who reads it. There are several risks that someone who files a malicious and groundless suit faces, and lawyers are aware of those risks and advise their clients about them.

and I would install them as soon as that occurred. The doors arrived yesterday and I am ready to install them at your convenience.

I already told you that I am ready to make the minor adjustments that the faucet needs and install special lightbulbs for the overhead recessed lights, as you requested. I plan to do that work when I install the shower doors.

Insofar as the floor tile is concerned, I feel terrible about the cracking tiles, but they are a problem you should take up with your architect. During one of the architect's visits before the floor was installed, I mentioned my concern that the tiles would be inappropriate for use on a bathroom floor. He told me not to worry and to be sure to install the precise tiles he had specified in the plans. I suspect that the tiles are too thin to bear the amount of weight being applied to them. The cracking you describe sounds like what can happen when pressure from the heel of a high-heeled shoe is applied to fragile tiles like the ones I was asked to install.

Please let me know when you want me to install the shower door and make the minor adjustments we agreed on earlier.

Sincerely,

Mark Rosso

81. Letter to company that has filed harmful credit information about you:

January 23, 2004

Certified Mail ❶
Return Receipt Requested

Mr. Jason Ridgely
Manager
XYZ Appliance Company
90270 Washburn Avenue
Chattanooga, Tennessee 00000

Dear Mr. Ridgely:

I am writing to inform you of a serious injury you have caused me.

As you can easily verify from your store's records, I have a dispute with you concerning furniture I purchased at your store. You will see from the correspondence in your files that I stopped my monthly payments four months ago because the furniture is literally falling apart. I understand that you have taken the position that I have no right to stop the payments. I have taken the position that I may do so because you sold me defective furniture. One way or another we are going to resolve that matter. What you have done with respect to injuring my credit, however, is absolutely unacceptable.

I have learned from my bank, in the course of seeking to procure a loan, that you have placed a bad credit report on my record with the major credit-reporting companies used by merchants and lenders all over this country. My bank has advised me that you indicated that I am a poor credit risk because I do not make monthly payments as required by my contract. Because of your action, I am unable to obtain a needed bank loan, and I assume other credit will be withheld from me.

ANALYSIS

1 This is a strong first letter but deservedly so, due to the seriousness of what has occurred. A letter like this should always be sent by certified mail, return receipt requested. The threat to "pursue damages" if the matter is not resolved is consistent with the serious tone.

ANALYSIS

When harmful credit information finds its way to one of the major credit reporting companies, it will be damaging to the person it concerns even if the information is arguable. You must be sure to follow up on bad credit reports when you learn of them, as Ms. Banks has. In a case like this, it is worth it to pay a small fee to acquire your own credit report so that you will be able to see precisely what others have said about you.

Although credit information is widely available to businesses, banks, and others, there are various legal restrictions on its appropriate use. If you feel that improper information has been provided to a credit bureau about you, or that someone is using the available information improperly, review that matter promptly with an attorney or state official.

I am writing to demand that you resolve this matter immediately by providing me and the credit-reporting companies with a letter indicating that my credit is good and that we are in dispute. If you do not do this, I will pursue your business for all of the damages that your action causes me, as well as the cost of restoring my good credit.

I expect to hear from you immediately with respect to what action you intend to take in this matter.

Sincerely,

Sarah S. Banks

82. Settlement agreement with landlord regarding repairs to apartment:

This is a settlement agreement letter. This kind of letter is important whenever you settle a matter and there are things to be done in the future. A settlement agreement letter should cover everything each side has agreed to do, and the order of things to be done if that is important. When you write such a letter, be sure that nothing significant is left out, because the signed settlement agreement letter will be your final and binding agreement to conclude the difficulty you have been having.

May 15, 2003

Certified Mail
Return Receipt Requested

Mr. Frank C. Steadman
1012 Bank Street
Jersey City, New Jersey 00000

Dear Mr. Steadman:

I am writing this letter to confirm the agreement we have reached about the apartment repairs we have been discussing for the last two months.

You agreed to immediately repair or replace the three steam radiators that are not working properly.

You also agreed to promptly paint the kitchen with a color we select to fix the stains that resulted from the (now fixed) leak in the apartment upstairs.

We agreed that as soon as you do these things we will pay you the two months' rent we have held in escrow and will continue to pay our rent on time for the 17 months that are left on the lease.

We also agreed to withdraw our lawsuit in landlord-tenant court when the repairs are finished.

My husband and I have both signed this letter, and we ask you to sign a copy of it and send it back to us for our records.

ANALYSIS

1 You can use the words "AGREED TO this_____ day of _____, 2_____," with a place for the other person to sign, when you want to confirm the other person's agreement to what you are saying. This is particularly important in settlement agreement letters because you hope they will end your difficulty.

ANALYSIS

If you ever are prepared to settle a matter and have any concern at all that by doing so you will be giving up something you may be unclear about, a brief consultation with a lawyer may be useful. Where something like a lease is involved, such as in this situation, it may be useful to add a sentence to the end of your settlement agreement letter that says something like: "By settling this difficulty with you, we are not giving up any of our other rights under the lease."

Sincerely,

Janet S. Smith

James L. Smith

AGREED TO this ____ day ❶
of _____, 2003

_____

Frank C. Steadman

83. Settlement agreement with automobile dealer regarding defective transmission:

April 10, 2003

<u>Certified Mail</u>
<u>Return Receipt Requested</u>

Mr. Hugo L. Winston
Sales Manager
Berkeley Boulevard Automobile Dealership
6000 Berkeley Boulevard
Berkeley, California 00000

Dear Mr. Winston:

We agreed in our conversation yesterday that you would immediately replace the transmission in our new car with a new transmission because three attempts to fix the original transmission have failed to make it work correctly.

I have told the consumer protection division of the attorney general's office that it is no longer necessary to have a hearing in this matter because you have agreed to replace the transmission at your expense. Mr. Steiner of the consumer protection division asked me to advise him when the transmission has been replaced and the car runs satisfactorily. I told him I would do that. ❶

As we discussed, I will bring the car to your service department next Monday morning at 8:00 A.M. and plan to pick it up between 5:00 and 6:00 P.M. on that day.

Sincerely,

William T. Black

cc: Mr. Barry Steiner ❷

84. Settlement agreement with roofer who installed defective roof:

November 24, 2003

<u>Certified Mail</u>
<u>Return Receipt Requested</u>

Mr. Charles J. Deering
President
Deering Bros. Roofing
23500 Johnson Boulevard
Williamsport, Maryland 00000

Dear Mr. Deering:

This letter states our agreement regarding the roof you installed on our house.

You have agreed to redo the flat part of this roof job, which goes over our sunroom addition. This room leaks in several places since you installed the new roof six months ago.

The other part of the roof that goes over the original house has a lot of pitch, and it has not leaked. The only problem with that part of the roof is with the drip edge on the north side. You agreed to replace that piece of drip edge and install it properly so that this won't happen again. ❶

For now, the new flat part of the roof and the new drip edge will be enough to solve our problems. We promised you that if there were no further difficulties we would not file a lawsuit or do anything else about the roof. ❷ It's important to us that this has no effect on the ten-year warranty we received on the entire roof. ❸ This agreement is based on what has happened so far, and the ten-year warranty will remain just as it was when the roof was completed.

This was a major expense for me and my wife, and we want to have a clear record of our understanding regarding how this difficulty will be handled. We enclose two originals of this letter; please sign them both and return one to us.

We understand that you will be here next week and are relying on that.

Sincerely,

Jason W. Wright

AGREED to this ____ day
of _____, 2003.

Deering Bros. Roofing

By: _____
     Charles J. Deering,
     President

Appendix A:
A Brief Guide to Small Claims Courts

If worse comes to worst, you can file and handle your own case in small claims court. The rules for handling a small claim vary from state to state. Here is a synopsis of each one:

ALABAMA. The small claims court is a special civil division of the district court where individuals as well as businesses can settle disputes and disagreements. The maximum amount you may sue or be sued for is $3,000. Procedures are simple, informal, and inexpensive. There are no juries, and you may appear before the judge with or without an attorney.

ALASKA. The district court is a trial court of limited jurisdiction. A district court judge may hear state misdemeanors and violations of city and borough ordinances; issue summonses, arrest warrants, and search warrants; hear first appearances and preliminary hearings in felony cases; record vital statistics (in some areas of the state); hear civil cases valued up to $50,000; hear small claims cases ($7,500 maximum); handle cases involving children on an emergency basis; hear domestic violence cases.

ARIZONA. Every justice of the peace court in Arizona has a small claims division, created by law, to provide an inexpensive and speedy method for resolving most civil disputes that do not exceed $2,500. Small claims cases are handled in a less formal manner than other court cases. Procedures are intended to be simple enough for a person to file a complaint or to answer a claim without a lawyer. All cases are heard by either a judge or hearing officer, who then makes a decision. The decision is final and binding on both parties. There is no right to a jury trial or an appeal in small claims cases. There are only three specific motions allowed by law in a small claims action. These are Request for Change of Venue (location), Request to Vacate a Judgment, and Request for Debtor's Examination.

The Superior Court presiding judge in each county appoints special hearing officers to decide small claims cases of less than $2,500. Small claims cases are decided before the judge or hearing officer. No attorneys are allowed to represent clients in these cases. Defendants who want to use an attorney may move the case from the small claims division to the civil division of the justice court.

ARKANSAS. The small claims court is a special civil division of the municipal court. Claims are limited to $5,000 or less. Each municipal court in Arkansas has a division known as a small claims court. Small claims courts are located in the same building and are served by the same personnel as municipal courts.

CALIFORNIA. Small claims court is part of the superior court. Most small claims disputes are about money damages under $5,000. But the small claims court also can order someone to do something, such as return a borrowed bicycle or lawn mower. Although you may consult with a lawyer outside the courtroom, you must argue your own case before a judge. The regular filing fee is $20 or $35, depending on the number of claims filed during a 12-month period. Cases are usually heard within 70 to 90 days after the forms are filed.

COLORADO. The county court civil division processes small claims that do not exceed $5,000. Each county has a district court. No plaintiff may file more than two claims per month or 18 claims per year in small claims courts. The small claims court is a "court of limited jurisdiction." This means that the court cannot award more than $7,500, even if your claim is worth more. You will have to waive your right to the amount that exceeds $7,500, or you will have to bring your claim in a different court. You may also be entitled to recover your court costs and interest. You cannot have a jury trial in small claims court. Under Colorado Revised Statute (C.R.S.) § 13-6-405(4), all claims are heard by a magistrate, unless one of the parties timely requests a judge hear the case or unless that particular court location does not have a magistrate. The small claims court cannot hear cases of libel or slander, eviction, traffic violations, or criminal matters. For a full list of prohibited claims, see C.R.S. § 13-6-402.

CONNECTICUT. A part of superior court where you can sue for amounts of up to $3,500.

DELAWARE. The justice of the peace court, the initial entry level into the court system for most citizens, has jurisdiction over civil cases in which the disputed amount is less than $15,000. In criminal cases, the justice of the peace court hears certain misdemeanors and most motor vehicle cases (excluding felonies), and the justices of the peace may act as committing magistrates for all crimes. Appeals from the justice of the peace court may be taken to the court of common pleas. Over one-half of all cases are disposed of rapidly at the justice of the peace court level without further impact on the remainder of the judicial system.

DISTRICT OF COLUMBIA. Superior Court of the District of Columbia, Small Claims and Conciliation Branch: The small claims clerk's office is located at the H. Carl Moultrie I Courthouse, 500 Indiana Avenue NW, Room JM-260, Washington DC 20001. Telephone number: 202-879-1120.

FLORIDA. If you have a financial disagreement with another person or company that does not exceed $5,000, there is a simple, quick, and inexpensive way to bring the matter before a judge and to get a ruling. This legal procedure is handled in the small claims division of the county court. The proceedings are informal. You may represent yourself. An attorney is not required.

GEORGIA. If you have been unable to resolve a dispute with a person or a business, you may take your problem to magistrate's court. Magistrate's court, also called small claims court, is an informal court that handles money claims for less than $15,000. This court offers a quick and inexpensive process for complaint resolution.

HAWAII. The small claims division (of the district court) may handle only cases for the recovery of money where the amount claimed is no more than $3,500.

IDAHO. The small claims departments are informal courts that people can use to sue for small amounts of money (up to $4,000) without a lawyer. Small claims departments are part of the magistrates division of the district court and a magistrate is the judge of the small claims department. Although they are official court cases, small claims hearings are designed to be quick and relaxed to allow consumers and businesspeople an inexpensive

method of settling minor claims.

ILLINOIS. In Illinois, the county circuit court processes small claims of $5,000 or less. The parties are not required to have lawyers but may choose to have one. Small claims court is under the jurisdiction of the Clerks of Courts Act (705 ILCS par. 105) and Supreme Court Rule 282. Fees are based on the population of the county and designated by county boards.

INDIANA. The small claims division of the superior court hears claims limited to $3,000 or less ($6,000 in Marion and Allen Counties). In Hamilton County, both Superior Court 4 and Superior Court 5 maintain dockets to handle small claims cases.

IOWA. The small claims division of the superior court hears claims limited to $4,000 or less.

KANSAS. The district court hears small claims actions. Amounts at issue are limited to $1,800. Lawyers are not allowed to represent parties in small claims proceedings prior to the entry of judgment.

KENTUCKY. The small claims division of the district court hears cases involving small claims under $1,500.

LOUISIANA. The city court hears small claims actions. Some eviction cases are heard in small claims court, if the rent at issue is sufficiently small. Amounts at issue are limited to $3,000 ($2,000 for movable property). Small claims court is a part of the civil division of the Baton Rouge City Court and was established pursuant to Louisiana Revised Statutes 13:5200–5212. You may sue to resolve minor civil disputes and to recover claims of up to $3,000. A claim, generally speaking, asserts a legal right you may have.

MAINE. The small claims court is a special civil division of the district court. Claims are limited to $4,500 or less.

MARYLAND. The district court processes small claim actions involving disputes under $2,500.

MASSACHUSETTS. Small claims are heard in every district court, in every housing court, and at the Boston Municipal Court. Small claims actions are limited to disputes under $2,000. Small claims sessions are conducted in every Massachusetts district court, the Boston Municipal Court, the Hampden County Housing Court, the Worcester Housing Court, and the Boston Housing Court. Each district court is formally identified by its county name and by a district number or region within the county.

MICHIGAN. You can sue for up to $3,000 in the small claims division of the district court. These matters are heard by the attorney/magistrate of the court.

MINNESOTA. The small claims court is part of the district court. Your claim may not exceed $7,500. The conciliation court can accept claims for filing that are below the limit set by Minnesota law. Currently, the monetary jurisdictional limit is $7,500. You cannot file a claim involving title to real estate, slander, class actions, or medical malpractice in conciliation court. You can reduce the amount of your claim so it can be heard in conciliation court. If you do reduce your claim, you will not be allowed to ask for more money later. You may not file any other claims related to the same incident. You should consider whether the defendant (the person the claim is against) will be able to pay you. Although you may win your case, conciliation court is not a collection agency.

MISSISSIPPI. You may sue in small claims court for up to $2,500.

MISSOURI. The small claims court of each county circuit court handles money or property disputes totaling $1,500 or less. Missouri circuit courts are courts of original civil and criminal jurisdiction. That is, cases usually begin in the circuit court, which is where trials may occur. Within the circuit court, there are various divisions, such as associate circuit, small claims, municipal, family, probate, criminal, and juvenile. Missouri's counties

and the city of St. Louis are organized into forty-five judicial circuits. There is a court in every county. The circuit court is typically in the county seat (or the city of St. Louis) and may be in additional locations in the county. The small claims court is a division of the circuit court presided over by an associate circuit judge.

MONTANA. Small claims courts are divisions of both the district court and justice of the peace. The justice court hears small claims actions of $3,000 or less.

NEBRASKA. Small claims court is a division of county court, and the hearings are conducted by a county judge. Small claims court is limited to civil (noncriminal) actions involving disputes over amounts of money owed, damage to property, or seeking the return of personal property. Judgments in small claims court may not exceed $2,400.

NEVADA. The small claims division of the county court hears small claims actions of $5,500 or less.

NEW HAMPSHIRE. Small claims court is not a separate court. Rather, it is a procedure available in district courts throughout the state and is sometimes referred to as a small claims session. A small claims action may not exceed $5,000.

NEW JERSEY. Small claims is one of three sections of the superior court's special civil part. The other two sections are landlord/tenant part and regular special civil part. Small claims handles cases in which the demand is not more than $2,000. If the amount of money you are trying to recover is more than $2,000 but less than $10,000, your case should be filed in the regular special civil part. Cases in which damages are more than $10,000 must be filed in the law division of the superior court.

NEW MEXICO. Claims up to $7,500 (not including court costs and interest) may be brought in the magistrate court.

NEW YORK. The maximum amount of a claim in a New York small claims court is $3,000. There is at least one small claims court in each of the 62 counties in New York state, including at least one in each of the five boroughs of New York City. In the City of New York, the small claims court is part of the Civil Court of the City of New York. In Nassau and Suffolk Counties, the district courts have small claims parts. All city courts have a small claims part. Town and village courts, with the exception of those located in Nassau County, handle small claims in the municipalities where they are located. Consult your telephone book for the address and telephone number of your local court and call that local court for information.

NORTH CAROLINA. Small claims courts exist in every county in North Carolina to help people solve disputes over small amounts of money or personal property quickly, easily, and without a lawyer. These county district courts can handle all such disputes in which no more than $4,000 in money or property is in dispute. The cases are tried before special judges called magistrates, usually within a month after the case is filed.

NORTH DAKOTA. The district court is authorized to hear small claims cases that do not exceed $5,000.

OHIO. Civil claims for $3,000 or less may be filed in small claims court. This court has very simple rules that allow parties to resolve disputes without hiring an attorney. However, attorneys are permitted to represent parties if desired. Small claims court is a division operating in each municipal and county court throughout Ohio. It provides a quick, informal, and inexpensive way of resolving many types of disputes you may have with particular individuals or companies. In most small claims courts, the proceedings are conducted by a referee instead of a judge. You are permitted (but not required) to be represented by an attorney, with the exception of corporations. Only licensed attorneys can provide legal representation to corporations in Ohio courts.

OKLAHOMA. The district court small claims division handles cases that do not exceed $4,500.

OREGON. The justice court has small claims civil jurisdiction (nonexclusive) where the money or damages claimed do not exceed $5,000, except in actions involving title to real property, false imprisonment, libel, slander, or malicious prosecution.

PENNSYLVANIA. District justice courts hear claims that do not exceed $8,000. The Municipal Court of Philadelphia may hear claims of $10,000 or less. It also may hear rent-only disputes in landlord-tenant cases of an unlimited amount.

RHODE ISLAND. The small claims courts handle cases that do not exceed $1,500.

SOUTH CAROLINA. Generally speaking, when the amount or value of property in dispute is less than $7,500 the matter is filed and heard in small claims court. Small claims cases are filed with one of the two small claims magistrates' courts in Charleston County. The small claims court in Charleston, located at 995 Morrison Drive, is open Monday through Friday from 8:30 A.M. to 5:00 P.M. The North Charleston Small Claims Court is located at 2144 Melbourne Drive, Room 103, and is open Monday through Friday from 8:30 A.M. to 5:00 P.M.

SOUTH DAKOTA. The small claims court is authorized to hear cases for $8,000 or less. However, since this limit is changed from time to time, it is suggested that the plaintiff (the person bringing the action to court) ask the clerk of court what maximum amount of claim is currently allowed by law. Generally, magistrate courts assist the circuit courts in processing minor criminal cases and less serious civil actions. Whether presided over by a lay magistrate or a magistrate judge, magistrate courts, as well as the circuit courts, perform marriages, receive depositions, issue warrants, conduct certain preliminary hearings, set bail, appoint counsel,

accept pleas for class 2 misdemeanors, and hear uncontested civil and small claims actions where the amount of money or damage does not exceed $8,000.

TENNESSEE. The court of general sessions hears small claims actions involving disputes for $15,000 or less. In counties of 700,000 or more people, the court hears small claims disputes for up to $25,000. However, there is no dollar limit for cases involving unlawful detainer and the recovery of personal property. If you have a claim or dispute with a person or company for $10,000 or less, and have asked the person or company for the money and they refuse to pay part or all of it, you can sue them in small claims court.

TEXAS. A justice court handles small claims under $5,000. In small claims court, only a suit for the recovery of money up to the $5,000 jurisdictional limit amount is permitted. It is an informal court and does not require the hiring of an attorney by any party. In justice civil court, suits may be for the recovery of money and/or other items—for example, the return of personal property—within the $5,000 jurisdiction of the court. It is a formal court, and all legal rules of evidence and procedure apply.

UTAH. A small claims department of the district court is designed to settle legal issues and problems arising from contractual or service disputes or other claims that do not exceed the sum of $5,000. A small claims court allows an individual or business to be compensated by a party who has not performed according to an agreement or who had committed some wrongdoing. (Small claims court is a department of the Utah District Court. Small claims are also handled in city and county justice courts, where the same rules apply.)

VERMONT. You can sue for up to $3,500 in small claims court, which is a special part of the Vermont Superior Court. If you think somebody owes you more than $3,500 you can sue in civil court, but the procedures are more complicated, time consuming, and expensive, and you will probably need a lawyer. If your claim is for more than $3,500 but you decide to sue in small claims court anyway, you give up your claim to any more than $3,500. You will usually want to sue in the court in the county where you live or do business.

VIRGINIA. The small claims divisions of the general district courts hear disputes of $1,000 or less. The general district courts themselves hear disputes of $3,000 or less. Cases involving amounts between $3,000 and $15,000 may be heard by either the general district court or the circuit court.

WASHINGTON. Any individual, business, partnership, or corporation (with a few exceptions) may bring a small claims suit for recovery of money only for an amount up to $4,000. In Washington State, the district court civil division processes small claims in amounts not exceeding $2,500. Each county has a district court. Small claims are not handled in municipal court.

WEST VIRGINIA. The magistrates courts handle small claims with $5,000 or less in dispute.

WISCONSIN. The district courts handle small claims of $5,000 or less. For landlords seeking eviction, the $5,000 limit does not apply.

WYOMING. The justice of the peace courts hear small claims of up to $3,000. Circuit courts hear cases of up to $7,000.

Appendix B:
Federal Agencies

AIRLINE SERVICE COMPLAINTS
Handles complaints about airline service.

Airline Service Complaints
Office of Intergovernmental and
  Consumer Affairs
400 7th Street, SW, Room 10215
Washington, DC 20590
202-366-4648 phone
202-366-9371 fax

**CIVIL RIGHTS DIVISION OF
THE DEPARTMENT OF JUSTICE**
Handles matters dealing with discrimination or offensive actions based on personal characteristics such as race.

Civil Rights Division
Department of Justice
10th Street and Constitution
  Avenue, NW, Room 5643
Washington, DC 20530
202-541-2151 phone
202-307-1379 fax

**CONSUMER INFORMATION
CENTER**
Publishes a free Consumer Information Catalog listing federal booklets on a variety of consumer topics. For a free copy of the catalog, contact:

Consumer Information Catalog
Pueblo, CO 81009
719-948-4000

**CONSUMER PRODUCT SAFETY
COMMISSION**
Handles complaints about consumer products other than cars, food, or drugs and distributes consumer education material.

Call or write:
U.S. Consumer Product Safety
  Commission
Washington, DC 20207
800-638-2772

DEPARTMENT OF LABOR
Handles matters related to employee rights and responsibilities.

200 Constitution Avenue, NW
Washington, DC 20210
866-487-2365

**FEDERAL BUREAU OF
INVESTIGATION**
Handles matters related to most federal crimes.

Federal Bureau of Investigation
J. Edgar Hoover Building
935 Pennsylvania Avenue, NW
Washington, DC 20535-0001
202-324-3000

**FEDERAL COMMUNICATIONS
COMMISSION**
Handles complaints about telephone systems, radio and television, and cable.

Complaints about telephone systems:

Federal Communications Commission
Consumer Information Bureau
Consumer Complaints
445 12th Street, SW
Washington, DC 20554
888-225-5322

Complaints about radio and television:

Mass Media Bureau
Complaints and Investigation
Federal Communications Commission
2025 M Street, NW, Room 8210
Washington, DC 20554
888-225-5322

Complaints about cable programming rates:

Federal Communications Commission
Cable Form Request 329
P.O. Box 18238
Washington, DC 20036
888-225-5322

FEDERAL TRADE COMMISSION

Handles matters that concern unfair trade practices and misleading representations.

The Federal Trade Commission
600 Pennsylvania Avenue, NW
Washington, DC 20580
202-326-2222

FOOD AND DRUG ADMINISTRATION

Handles matters dealing with foods and drugs.

Call: 301-443-1240.

NATIONAL HIGHWAY TRAFFIC SAFETY ADMINISTRATION

Handles complaints about safety of vehicles, child safety seats, and other motor vehicle equipment.

Auto Safety Hotline
National Highway Traffic Safety Administration
Department of Transportation
Washington, DC 20590
202-366-0123
800-424-9393

POSTAL CRIME HOTLINE

Handles mail fraud and other consumer problems.

Call: 800-654-8896.

U.S. CUSTOMS

Handles fraudulent import and export practices. To report fraudulent practices, call 800-ITS-FAKE.

Appendix C: State Agencies
Consumer Protection

Consumer Affairs Division Chief
Office of the Attorney General
11 South Union Street
Montgomery, AL 36130
334-242-7334
Toll free in AL: 800-392-5658
Web site: www.ago.state.al.us

Consumer Protection Unit
Office of the Attorney General
1031 West 4th Avenue, Suite 200
Anchorage, AK 99501-5903
907-269-5100
Fax: 907-276-8554
Web site: www.law.state.ak.us

Consumer Protection and Advocacy Section
Office of the Attorney General
1275 West Washington Street
Phoenix, AZ 85007
602-542-3702
602-542-5763 (consumer
   information and complaints)
Toll free in AZ: 800-352-8431
TDD: 602-542-5002
Fax: 602-542-4579
Web site: www.ag.state.az.us

Consumer Protection Division
Office of the Attorney General
400 West Congress South
   Building, Suite 315
Tucson, AZ 85701
520-628-6504
Toll free in AZ: 800-352-8431
Fax: 520-628-6532

Consumer Protection Division
Office of the Attorney General
323 Center Street, Suite 200
Little Rock, AR 72201
501-682-2341
Voice/TDD toll free in AR:
   800-482-8982
Toll free: 800-482-8982
TDD: 501-682-6073
Fax: 501-682-8118
E-mail: consumer@ag.state.ar.us
Web site: www.ag.state.ar.us

California Department of Consumer Affairs
400 R Street, Suite 3000
Sacramento, CA 95814
916-445-4465
Toll free in CA: 800-952-5210
TDD/TTY: 916-322-1700
Web site: www.dca.ca.gov

Bureau of Automotive Repair
California Department of
  Consumer Affairs
10240 Systems Parkway
Sacramento, CA 95827
916-255-4565
Toll free in CA: 800-952-5210
  (auto repair only)
TDD: 916-255-1369
Web site: www.smogcheck.ca.gov

Office of the Attorney General
Public Inquiry Unit
P.O. Box 944255
Sacramento, CA 94244-2550
916-322-3360
Toll free in CA: 800-952-5225
TDD: 916-324-5564
Web site: www.caag.state.ca.us/
  piu

COLORADO
Consumer Protection Division
Colorado Attorney General's
  Office
1525 Sherman Street, 5th Floor
Denver, CO 80203-1760
303-866-5189
303-866-5125
Toll free: 800-332-2071
Fax: 303-866-5443

CONNECTICUT
Antitrust/Consumer Protection
Office of the Attorney General
110 Sherman Street
Hartford, CT 06105
860-808-5400
Fax: 860-808-5593
Web site: www.cslnet.ctstateu.
  edu/attygenl

**Department of Consumer
Protection**
165 Capitol Avenue
Hartford, CT 06106
860-713-6050
Toll free in CT: 800-842-2649
Fax: 860-566-1531
Web site: www.state.ct.us/dcp/

DELAWARE
**Fraud and Consumer
Protection Division**
Office of the Attorney General
820 North French Street, 5th Floor
Wilmington, DE 19801
302-577-8600
Toll free in DE: 800-220-5424
Fax: 302-577-3090
Web site: www.state.de.us/
  attgen/consumer.htm

Consumer Protection Unit
Director, Consumer Protection
  Division
Department of Justice
820 North French Street, 5th Floor
Wilmington, DE 19801
302-577-8600
Toll free in DE: 800-220-5424
Fax: 302-577-3090
Web site: www.state.de.us/
  attgen/consumer.htm

DISTRICT OF COLUMBIA
**Office of the Corporation
Counsel**
441 4th Street NW, Suite 450-N
Washington, DC 20001
202-442-9828 (consumer hotline)
Fax: 202-727-6546

Economic Crimes Division
Office of the Attorney General
110 SE 6th Street
Republic Tower, 10th Floor
Fort Lauderdale, FL 33301
954-712-4600
Fax: 954-712-4658
Web site: www.legal.firn.edu

Chief of Multi-State Litigation
Consumer Litigation Section
110 SE 6th Street
Fort Lauderdale, FL 33301
954-712-4600
Fax: 954-712-4706

Director of Division Consumer Services
Department of Agriculture &
    Consumer Services
407 South Calhoun Street
Mayo Building, 2nd Floor
Tallahassee, FL 32399-0800
850-922-2966
Toll free in FL: 800-435-7352
Fax: 850-487-4177
Web site: www.fl-ag.com

GEORGIA

Administrator, Governor's Office of Consumer Affairs
2 Martin Luther King Jr. Drive,
    Suite 356
Atlanta, GA 30334
404-651-8600
Toll free in GA (outside Atlanta
    area): 800-869-1123
Fax: 404-651-9018
Web site: www2.state.ga.us/
    gaoca

HAWAII

Office of Consumer Protection
Department of Commerce and
    Consumer Affairs
345 Kekuananoa Street, Room 12
Hilo, HI 96720
808-933-0910
Fax: 808-933-8845

Office of Consumer Protection
Department of Commerce and
    Consumer Affairs
235 South Beretania Street,
    Room 801
Honolulu, HI 96813
808-586-2636
Fax: 808-586-2640

Office of Consumer Protection
Department of Commerce and
    Consumer Affairs
1063 L Main Street, Suite C-216
Wailuku, Maui, HI 96793
808-984-8244
Fax: 808-243-5807
Web site: www.state.hi.us/dcca/

IDAHO

Consumer Protection Unit
Idaho Attorney General's Office
650 West State Street
Boise, ID 83720-0010
208-334-2424
Toll free in ID: 800-432-3545
Fax: 208-334-2830
Web site: www.state.id.us/ag

ILLINOIS

Office of the Attorney General
1001 East Main Street
Carbondale, IL 62901
618-529-6400
Toll free in IL: 800-243-0607
(consumer hotline serving
southern Illinois)
TDD: 618-529-0607
Fax: 618-529-6416

Consumer Fraud Bureau
100 West Randolph, 12th Floor
Chicago, IL 60601
312-814-3580
Toll free in IL: 800-386-5438
TDD: 312-814-3374
Fax: 312-814-2593
Web site: www.ag.state.il.us

Consumer Protection Division of the Attorney General's Office
100 West Randolph, 12th Floor
Chicago, IL 60601
312-814-3000
TDD: 312-793-2852
Fax: 312-814-2593

Governor's Office of Citizens' Assistance
222 South College, Room 106
Springfield, IL 62706
217-782-0244
Toll free in IL: 800-642-3112
Fax: 217-524-4049
E-mail: governor@state.il.us

INDIANA

Consumer Protection Division
Office of the Attorney General
Indiana Government Center
South
402 West Washington Street,
5th Floor
Indianapolis, IN 46204
317-232-6330
Toll free in IN: 800-382-5516
Fax: 317-233-4393
E-mail: inattgn@atg.state.in.us
Web site:
www.ai.org/hoosieradvocate

IOWA

Consumer Protection Division
Office of the Attorney General
1300 East Walnut Street,
2nd Floor
Des Moines, IA 50319
515-281-5926
Fax: 515-281-6771
E-mail: consumer@ag.state.ia.us
Web site: www.state.ia.us/
government/ag/consumer.html

KANSAS

Consumer Protection Division
Office of the Attorney General
120 SW 10th, 4th Floor
Topeka, KS 66612-1597
785-296-3751
Toll free in KS: 800-432-2310
TDD/TTY: 785-291-3767
Fax: 785-291-3699
E-mail: cprotect@ksag.org
Web site: www.ink.org/public/
ksag

Office of the District Attorney
Consumer Fraud and Economic
  Crime Division
535 North Main
Wichita, KS 67203-3747
316-383-7921
Toll free in KS: 800-432-2310
Fax: 316-383-4669

Consumer Protection Division
Office of the Attorney General
1024 Capital Center Drive
Frankfort, KY 40601
502-696-5389
Toll free in KY: 888-432-9257
Fax: 502-573-8317
E-mail: attorney.general@
  law.state.ky.us
Web site: www.law.state.ky.us/cp

Consumer Protection Division
Office of the Attorney General
9001 Shelbyville Road, Suite 3
Louisville, KY 40222
502-425-4825
Fax: 502-425-9406

Consumer Protection Section
Office of the Attorney General
301 Main Street, Suite 1250
Baton Rouge, LA 70801
225-342-9639
Toll free nationwide: 800-351-4889
Fax: 225-342-9637
Web site: www.laag.com

**Maine Attorney General's
Consumer Mediation Service**
6 State House Station
Augusta, ME 04333
207-626-8800
Web site: www.state.me.us/ag

Public Protection Division
Office of the Attorney General
6 State House Station
Augusta, ME 04333
207-626-8849

**Office of Consumer Credit
Regulation**
35 State House Station
Augusta, ME 04333-0035
207-624-8527
Toll free in ME: 800-332-8529
TDD/TTY: 207-624-8563
Web site:
  www.mainecreditreg.org

Consumer Protection Division
Office of the Attorney General
200 Saint Paul Place, 16th Floor
Baltimore, MD 21202-2021
410-528-8662 (consumer
  complaint hotline)
410-576-6550 (consumer
  information)
TDD: 410-576-6372 (Maryland
  only)
Fax: 410-576-7040
E-mail: consumer@
  oag.state.md.us
Web site: www.oag.state.md.us/
  consumer

Business Licensing and Consumer Service
Motor Vehicle Administration
6601 Ritchie Highway, NE
Glen Burnie, MD 21062
410-768-7248
Fax: 410-768-7602

Consumer Protection and Antitrust Division
Office of the Attorney General
200 Portland Street
Boston, MA 02114
617-727-8400 (consumer hotline information and referral to local county and city government consumer offices that work in conjunction with the Department of the Attorney General)
Fax: 617-727-5765
Web site: www.ago.state.ma.us

Executive Office of Consumer Affairs and Business Regulation
One Ashburton Place, Room 1411
Boston, MA 02108
617-727-7780 (information and referral only)
TDD/TTY: 617-727-1729
Fax: 617-227-6094
E-mail: consumer@state.ma.us
Web site: www.state.ma.us/consumer

Consumer Protection and Antitrust Division
Office of the Attorney General—Springfield
436 Dwight Street
Springfield, MA 01103
413-784-1240
Fax: 413-784-1244

Consumer Protection Division
Office of the Attorney General
P.O. Box 30213
Lansing, MI 48909
517-373-1140 (complaint information)
517-373-1110
Fax: 517-335-1935

Bureau of Automotive Regulation
Michigan Department of State
Lansing, MI 48918-1200
517-373-4777
Toll free in MI: 800-292-4204
Fax: 517-373-0964

Consumer Services Division
Minnesota Attorney General's Office
1400 NCL Tower
445 Minnesota Street
St. Paul, MN 55101
651-296-3353
Toll free: 800-657-3787
Fax: 612-282-5801
E-mail: consumer.ag@state.mn.us
Web site: www.ag.state.mn.us/consumer

Consumer Protection Division of the Mississippi Attorney General's Office
P.O. Box 22947
Jackson, MS 39225-2947
601-359-4230
Toll free in MS: 800-281-4418
Fax: 601-359-4231
Web site: www.ago.state.ms.us/
consprot.htm

Bureau of Regulatory Services
Department of Agriculture and
Commerce
121 North Jefferson Street
P.O. Box 1609
Jackson, MS 39201
601-359-1111
Fax: 601-354-6502
Web site: www.mdac.state.ms.us

Consumer Protection and Trade Offense Division
P.O. Box 899
1530 Rax Court
Jefferson City, MO 65102
573-751-6887
573-751-3321
Toll free in MO: 800-392-8222
TDD/TTY toll free in MO: 800-
729-8668
Fax: 573-751-7948
E-mail: attgenmail@moago.org
Web site: www.ago.state.mo.us

Consumer Affairs Unit
Department of Commerce
1424 Ninth Avenue
Box 200501
Helena, MT 59620-0501
406-444-4312
Fax: 406-444-2903

Department of Justice
2115 State Capitol
P.O. Box 98920
Lincoln, NE 68509
402-471-2682
Toll free: 800-727-6432
Fax: 402-471-3297
Web site: www.nol.org

Bureau of Consumer Protection
555 East Washington Avenue,
Suite 3900
Las Vegas, NV 89101
702-486-3420

Nevada Consumer Affairs Division
1850 East Sahara, Suite 101
Las Vegas, NV 89104
702-486-7355
Toll free: 800-326-5202
TDD: 702-486-7901
Fax: 702-486-7371
E-mail: ncad@fyiconsumer.org
Web site: www.fyiconsumer.org

Consumer Affairs Division
Department of Business and
Industry
4600 Kietzke Lane, Building B,
Suite 113
Reno, NV 89502
775-688-1800
Toll free in NV: 800-326-5202
TDD: 775-486-7901
Fax: 775-688-1803

NEW HAMPSHIRE
**Consumer Protection and
Antitrust Bureau**
New Hampshire Attorney
General's Office
33 Capitol Street
Concord, NH 03301
603-271-3641
TDD toll free: 800-735-2964
Fax: 603-271-2110
Web site: www.state.nh.us/
nhdoj/Consumer/cpb.html

NEW JERSEY
New Jersey Division of Law
P.O. Box 45029
124 Halsey Street, 5th Floor
Newark, NJ 07101
973-648-3453
Fax: 201-648-3879
E-mail: jacobcar@law.dol.lps.
state.nj.us

**New Jersey Consumer Affairs
Division**
124 Halsey Street
P.O. Box 43027
Newark, NJ 07102
973-504-6587
973-648-6381
Fax: 973-648-3538
E-mail:
browere@smtp.lps.state.nj.us
Web site: www.state.nj.us/lps/
ca/home.htm

NEW MEXICO
Consumer Protection Division
Office of the Attorney General
P.O. Drawer 1508
407 Galisteo
Santa Fe, NM 87504-1508
505-827-6060
Toll free in NM: 800-678-1508
Fax: 505-827-6685
Web site: www.ago.state.nm.us

NEW YORK
**Bureau of Consumer Frauds
and Protection**
Office of the Attorney General
State Capitol
Albany, NY 12224
518-474-5481
Toll free in NY: 800-771-7755
(hotline)
Fax: 518-474-3618
Web site: www.oag.state.ny.us

New York State Consumer Protection Board
5 Empire State Plaza, Suite 2101
Albany, NY 12223-1556
518-474-3514
518-474-8583 (capital region)
Toll free: 800-697-1220
Fax: 518-474-2474
E-mail: donna.ned@consumer.
state.ny.us
Web site: www.consumer.state.
ny.us

Consumer Frauds and Protection Bureau
Office of the Attorney General
120 Broadway, 3rd Floor
New York, NY 10271
212-416-8300
Toll free: 800-771-7755
Fax: 212-416-6003

Consumer Frauds and Protection Bureau
New York State Office of the
Attorney General
Harlem Regional Office
163 West 125th Street
New York, NY 10027-8201
212-961-4475
Fax: 212-961-4003

Consumer Protection Section
Office of the Attorney General
P.O. Box 629
Raleigh, NC 27602
919-716-6000
Fax: 919-716-6050
Web site: www.jus.state.nc.us/
cpframe.htm

Consumer Protection and Antitrust Division
Office of the Attorney General
600 East Boulevard Avenue,
Department 125
Bismarck, ND 58505-0040
701-328-3404
Toll free in ND: 800-472-2600
TDD: 701-328-3409
Fax: 701-328-3535
E-mail: cpat@state.nd.us
Web site: www.ag.state.nd.us/
ndag/cpat/cpat.html

Office of the Attorney General
600 East Boulevard Avenue
Department 125
Bismarck, ND 58505-0040
701-328-2210
TDD 701-328-3409
Fax: 701-328-2226
E-mail: ndag@state.nd.us
Web site: www.ag.state.nd.us

Ohio Attorney General's Office
30 East Broad Street, 25th Floor
Columbus, OH 43215-3428
614-466-8831
Toll free in OH: 800-282-0515
TDD: 614-466-1393
Fax: 614-728-7583
E-mail: consumer@ag.state.oh.us
Web site: www.ag.state.oh.us

Ohio Consumers' Counsel
77 South High Street, 15th Floor
Columbus, OH 43266-0550
614-466-8574 (outside OH)
Toll free in OH: 877-PICK-OCC
    (877-742-5622)
E-mail: occ@occ.state.oh.us
Web site: www.state.oh.us/cons/

**Department of Consumer
Credit**
4545 North Lincoln Boulevard,
    #104
Oklahoma City, OK 73105
405-521-3653
Fax: 405-521-6740

Oklahoma Attorney General
4545 North Lincoln Avenue,
    Suite 260
Oklahoma City, OK 73105
405-521-3921
Toll free: 800-448-4904
Fax: 405-521-6740
Web site: www.oag.state.ok.us

Consumer Protection Division
Office of the Attorney General
440 South Houston, Suite 505
Tulsa, OK 74127-8913
918-581-2885
Web site: www.oag.state.ok.us

**Financial Fraud/Consumer
Protection Section**
Department of Justice
1162 Court Street, NE
Salem, OR 97310
503-378-4732
503-378-4320 (hotline Salem only)
503-229-5576 (hotline Portland
    only)
Toll free in OR: 877-877-9392
TDD/TTY: 503-378-5939
Fax: 503-378-5017
Web site: www.doj.state.or.us

**Office of the Consumer
Advocate**
Office of the Attorney General
Forum Place, 5th Floor
Harrisburg, PA 17101-1921
717-783-5048 (utilities only)
Toll free in PA: 800-684-6560
Fax: 717-783-7152
E-mail: paoca@ptd.net
Web site: www.oca.state.pa.us

**Bureau of Consumer
Protection**
Office of Attorney General
Strawberry Square, 14th Floor
Harrisburg, PA 17120
717-787-9707
Toll free in PA: 800-441-2555
Fax: 717-787-1190
Web site:
    www.attorneygeneral.gov

Consumer Unit
Consumer Protection Unit
Department of the Attorney
    General
150 South Main Street
Providence, RI 02903
401-274-4400
Toll free in RI: 800-852-7776
TDD: 401-453-0410
Fax: 401-222-5110

**Office of Executive Policy
and Program**
1205 Pendleton Street, Room 308
Columbia, SC 29201
803-734-0457
Toll free in SC only: 800-686-0040
Fax: 803-734-0546
Web site: www.state.sc.us

Office of the Attorney General
P.O. Box 11549
Columbia, SC 29211
803-734-3970
Fax: 803-734-3677
Web site:
    www.scattorneygeneral.org

**South Carolina Department of
Consumer Affairs**
2801 Devine Street
P.O. Box 5757
Columbia, SC 29205-5757
803-734-9452
Toll free in SC: 800-922-1594
Fax: 803-734-9365
E-mail: scdca@infoave.net
Web site: www.state.sc.us/
    consumer

Office of the Attorney General
500 East Capitol
State Capitol Building
Pierre, SD 57501-5070
605-773-4400
Toll free in SD: 800-300-1986
TDD: 605-773-6585
Fax: 605-773-7163

Division of Consumer Affairs
500 James Robertson Parkway,
    5th Floor
Nashville, TN 37243-0600
615-741-4737
Toll free in TN: 800-342-8385
Fax: 615-532-4994
E-mail: mwilliams2@mail.state.
    tn.us
Web site: www.state.tn.us/
    consumer

**Division of Consumer
Protection**
Tennessee Attorney General
425 Fifth Avenue North,
    2nd Floor
Nashville, TN 37243-0491
615-741-1671
Fax: 615-532-2910

Consumer Protection Division
Office of the Attorney General
P.O. Box 12548
Austin, TX 78711-2548
512-463-2070
Fax: 512-463-8301

Consumer Protection/Austin Regional Office
P.O. Box 12548
Austin, TX 78711-2548
512-463-2185
Fax: 512-463-8301
Web site: www.oag.state.tx.us

Office of Public Insurance Counsel
333 Guadalupe, Suite 3-120
Austin, TX 78701
512-322-4143
Fax: 512-322-4148
E-mail: rod.bordelon@mail.
    capnet.state.tx.us
Web site: www.opic.state.tx.us

Consumer Protection, Houston Regional Office
Office of the Attorney General
808 Travis, Suite 812
Houston, TX 77002
713-223-5886, ext. 118
Fax: 713-223-5821
E-mail: john.owens@oag.
    state.tx.us

UTAH

Division of Consumer Protection
Department of Commerce
160 East 300 South
Box 146704
Salt Lake City, UT 84114-6704
801-530-6601
Fax: 801-530-6001
E-mail: commerce@br.state.ut.us
Web site: www.commerce.state.
    ut.us

VERMONT

Consumer Assistance Program for Consumer Complaints and Questions
104 Morrill Hall
UVM
Burlington, VT 05405
802-656-3183 (within Chittenden
    County or out of state)
Toll free in VT: 800-649-2424

Consumer Assurance Section, Food and Market
Department of Agriculture
116 State Street
Montpelier, VT 05602
802-828-3456
Fax: 802-828-2361

Public Protection Division
Office of the Attorney General
109 State Street
Montpelier, VT 05609-1001
802-828-5507
Web site: www.state.vt.us/atg

VIRGINIA

Office of Consumer Affairs
Department of Agriculture and
    Consumer Services
Washington Building, Suite 100
P.O. Box 1163
Richmond, VA 23219
804-786-2042
Toll free in VA: 800-552-9963
TDD: 800-828-1120
Fax: 804-371-7479
Web site: www.vdacs.state.va.us

Office of the Attorney General
Antitrust and Consumer
    Litigation Section
900 East Main Street
Richmond, VA 23219
804-786-2116
Toll free: 800-451-1525
Fax: 804-786-0122
E-mail: mail@oag.state.va.us
Web site: www.cns.state.va.us/
    oag

WASHINGTON

Consumer Resource Center
Office of the Attorney General
103 East Holly Street, Suite 308
Bellingham, WA 98225-4728
360-738-6185

Consumer Resource Center
Office of the Attorney General
500 North Morain Street,
    Suite 1250
Kennewick, WA 99336-2607
509-734-2967

Consumer Resource Center
Office of the Attorney General
905 Plum Street, Building 3
P.O. Box 40118
Olympia, WA 98504-0118
360-753-6210

Consumer Resource Center
Office of the Attorney General
900 Fourth Avenue, Suite 2000
Seattle, WA 98164-1012
206-464-6684
Toll free in WA: 800-551-4636
    (Consumer Resource Centers)
Toll free TDD in WA:
    800-276-9883
Fax: 206-464-6451
Web site: www.wa.gov/ago

Consumer Resource Center
Office of the Attorney General
1116 West Riverside Avenue
Spokane, WA 99201-1194
509-456-3123

Consumer Resource Center
Office of the Attorney General
Consumer Protection Division
1019 Pacific Avenue, 3rd Floor
Tacoma, WA 98402-4411
253-593-2904
Toll free: 800-551-4636
Toll free in WA: 800-276-9883
Fax: 253-593-2449
E-mail: cynthial@atg.wa.gov
Web site: www.wa.gov/ago

WEST VIRGINIA

Consumer Protection Division
Office of the Attorney General
812 Quarrier Street, 6th Floor
P.O. Box 1789
Charleston, WV 25326-1789
304-558-8986
Toll free in WV: 800-368-8808
Fax: 304-558-0184
E-mail: consumer@wvnet.edu
Web site: www.state.wv.us/
    wvag/index0816.html

**Division of Weights and
Measures Section**
570 MacCorkle Avenue
St. Albans, WV 25177
304-722-0602
Fax: 304-722-0605
E-mail: angellk@mail.wvnet.edu

**Division of Trade and
Consumer Protection**
Department of Agriculture
3610 Oakwood Hills Parkway
Eau Claire, WI 54701-7754
715-839-3848
Toll free in WI: 800-422-7128
Fax: 715-839-1645

**Wisconsin Department of
Agriculture, Trade and
Consumer Protection**
200 North Jefferson Street,
    Suite 146-A
Green Bay, WI 54301
920-448-5111
920-448-5114
Toll free in WI: 800-422-7128
Fax: 920-448-5118
Web site: www.badger.state.wi.
    us/agencies/datcp

**Division of Trade and
Consumer Protection**
Department of Agriculture
2811 Agriculture Drive
P.O. Box 8911
Madison, WI 53708
608-224-4953
Toll free in WI: 800-422-7128
TTD/TTY: 608-224-5058
Fax: 608-224-4939
E-mail: datcphotline@wheel.
    datcp.state.wi.us
Web site: www.datcp.state.wi.us

WYOMING
Office of the Attorney General
Consumer Protection Unit
123 State Capitol Building
Cheyenne, WY 82002
307-777-7874
Toll free in WY: 800-438-5799
Fax: 307-777-7956
E-mail: cpetri@state.wy.us
Web site: www.state.wy.us/~ag/
    consumer.htm

Appendix C:
Independent Review Panels for Health Claims Decisions

State	Name, Address, and Phone Number of Regulating Agency	When Review Is Provided	Binding on Whom?
Alabama	*no state review board provided	–	–
Alaska	*no state review board provided	–	–
Arizona	Arizona Department of Insurance 2910 North 44th Street Suite 210 Phoenix, AZ 85108 Voice: 602-912-8444 Fax: 602-954-7008	Within 30 days after adverse decision by the health insurer at the insurer's internal formal appeals level, enrollee may request state review of adverse claims based on medical necessity and/or covered service.	On the insurer *and* the insured. However, court review of decision is provided.
Arkansas	*Currently there is no right to state review, but there is apparently a plan to present a bill regarding State review panels during the Arkansas General Assembly, which is in session as of the writing of this entry.	–	–

*Check with state regulatory authorities to see if a state review process has been implemented.

State	Name, Address, and Phone Number of Regulating Agency	When Review Is Provided	Binding on Whom?
California	California Department of Managed Healthcare (determines whether a case warrants review by the independent panel) HMO Help Center, IMR Unit 980 Ninth Street, Suite 500 Sacramento, CA 95814-2725 Voice: 1-888-HMO-2219 Fax: 916-229-4328	In any case in which an enrollee or provider asserts that a decision to deny, modify, or delay health care services was based, in whole or in part, on consideration of medical necessity.	Binding on the insurer.
Colorado	Colorado Division of Insurance (commissioner certifies independent state review entities) 1560 Broadway, Suite 850 Denver, CO 80202 Voice: 303-894-7499 or 800-894-3745 Fax: 301-894-7455	Within 60 days after a carrier's final denial—after exhaustion of carrier's internal review procedures, enrollee may request state review of any adverse decision.	Binding on the carrier *and* the covered person.
Connecticut	Connecticut Insurance Department P.O. Box 816 Hartford, CT 06142-0816 Voice: 860-297-3800 Fax: 860-566-7410	Insureds covered by a managed health care plan may file for state review within 30 days after exhausting internal review procedures. May only appeal decisions based upon medical necessity.	Binding on the insurer *and* the insured.

State	Name, Address, and Phone Number of Regulating Agency	When Review Is Provided	Binding on Whom?
Delaware	Office of Health Facilities, Licensing and Certification (part of Health and Social Services) 2055 Limestone Road, Suite 200 Wilmington, DE 19808 Voice: 302-995-8521 Fax: 302-995-8529	Within 60 days after exhaustion of health care carrier's internal review process, enrollee may request state review by an independent utilization review organization. May only appeal decisions based upon medical necessity.	Binding on the insurer, but insurer may appeal decision in court. Decision gives rise to rebuttable presumption vs. insured.
District of Columbia	District of Columbia Department of Health Grievance and Appeals Coordinator Office of the General Counsel Attn: Patrick Kelly 825 North Capitol Street, NE Room 4119 Washington, DC 20002 Voice: 202-442-5979	Any person enrolled in a health benefits plan may request formal state independent review of an insurer's decision to deny, termi-nate, or limit coverage— but only within 30 days after the insurer's inter-nal formal appeals process is exhausted.	Decision is non-binding on all par-ties and, by law, "shall not affect any other legal causes of action."
Florida	The Statewide Provider and Subscriber Assistance Program (a division of the Florida Agency for Health Care Administration). 2727 Mahan Drive, Ft. Knox #1 Suite 339 Tallahassee, FL 32308 Voice: 888-419-3456, 850-921-5458 Fax: 850-413-0900	After completing the entire internal grievance process provided by a health insurer, enrollee may request state review denials based on medical necessity.	Binding on the insurer.

State	Name, Address, and Phone Number of Regulating Agency	When Review Is Provided	Binding on Whom?
Georgia	Health Planning Agency 2 Peachtree Street, NW, Suite 34.262 Atlanta, GA 30303 Voice: 404-656-0655 Fax: 404-656-0654	After exhaustion of a health care plan's grievance procedure, if the enrollee is denied coverage based on medical necessity or that the treatment is "experimental," independent review is available.	Binding on the insurer. A decision unfavorable to enrollee creates a rebuttable presumption that insurer's decision to deny was proper.
Hawaii	State of Hawaii Insurance Division (insurance commissioner appoints the 3-member state review panel) P.O. Box 3614 Honolulu, HI 96811-3614 Voice: 808-586-2790	After exhausting all of an insurer's internal review and appeal procedures, an enrollee may request state review of any medical determination.	The law is unclear.
Idaho	*no state review board provided	—	—
Illinois	Illinois Department of Insurance (oversees compliance with the law, although it does not appoint state reviewers) 320 West Washington Street Springfield, IL 62767-0001 Voice: 217-782-4515 Fax: 217-782-5020	Within 30 days after denial of coverage for any claim, an enrollee may file a request with the health plan for state independent review. The health insurer then has 30 days to "provide a mechanism for joint selection of a state independent reviewer by the enrollee, the enrollee's physician or other health care provider, and the health care plan."	The statute states that the decision is "final" and that it is binding on a health care insurer. It is silent as to the enrollee.

State	Name, Address, and Phone Number of Regulating Agency	When Review Is Provided	Binding on Whom?
Indiana	Indiana Department of Insurance Health Issues Division (certifies state review organizations) 311 West Washington Street, Suite 300 Indianapolis, IN 46204-2787 Voice: 317-232-2385 Fax: 317-232-5251	Statute applies to HMOs only. HMOs must establish their own state grievance procedure for denials that state that a proposed treatment is not medically necessary or is experimental or investigational. The department certifies each state review organization and maintains a list of the ones to be used by HMOs.	Binding only on the HMO.
Iowa	Iowa Insurance Division (commissioner of insurance certifies the independent reviewers and certifies requests for independent reviews) 330 Maple Street Des Moines, IA 50319-0065 Voice: 515-281-5705 Fax: 515-281-3059	Within 60 days after denial of coverage, enrollee may seek state review of health insurer's adverse decision based on medical necessity.	Decision binding on insurer. Enrollee has 15 days to file a request for judicial review after reviewer's decision is made.
Kansas	Kansas Insurance Department (insurance commissioner enters into contracts with "eligible" state review organizations) 420 SW Ninth Street Topeka, KS 66612-1678 Voice: 785-296-3071 Fax: 785-296-2283	Within 90 days after a final adverse decision by the insurer based on medical necessity or the experimental nature of the proposed treatment, the enrollee may request state review.	Insurer and enrollee may both request judicial review of decision (reviewed de novo).

State	Name, Address, and Phone Number of Regulating Agency	When Review Is Provided	Binding on Whom?
Kentucky	Kentucky Department of Insurance 215 West Main Street Frankfort, KY 40601 Voice: 502-564-3630 Fax: 502-564-1650	Within 60 days after final determination by insurer based on medical necessity or the experimental nature of the proposed treatment, enrollee may request state review.	Binding on the insurer.
Louisiana	Louisiana Department of Insurance 950 North Fifth Street Baton Rouge, LA 70804-9214 Voice: 225-342-5900	Within 60 days after exhausting all of the insurer's internal appeals, enrollee may seek state review of a denial based on medical necessity, appropriateness, health care setting, level of care, or effectiveness.	Binding on the insurer and the insured. Law also provides a course of action to enrollee in cases of bad faith by insurer.
Maine	Maine Bureau of Insurance State House Station 34 Augusta, ME 04333-0034 Voice: 207-624-8474 Fax: 207-624-8599	Within 12 months after an adverse determination based on medical necessity, preexisting condition, or experimental procedure, an enrollee may request state independent review.	Binding on the insurer. Enrollee may not seek another review of same matter.
Maryland	Maryland Insurance Commission Appeals and Grievances Division 525 Saint Paul Place Baltimore, MD 21202 Voice: 410-468-2000 Fax: 410-468-2020	Within 30 days after exhaustion of a health insurer's internal appeals process, enrollee may appeal final adverse determination. Unique to Maryland: the insurance commissioner actually makes the decision but may, at his discretion, seek the advice of an independent review organization or medical expert in cases involving a decision to deny based on medical necessity.	Binding on the insurer. Enrollee may request a hearing before an administrative law judge.

State	Name, Address, and Phone Number of Regulating Agency	When Review Is Provided	Binding on Whom?
Massachu-setts	Massachusetts Department of Public Health Office of Patient Protection (office is required to establish or contract at least three state and independent review agencies) Voice: 800-436-7757	Enrollee who has exhausted all formal attorney grievance procedures of an insurer may request state review.	Binding on the insurer, but enrollee may still pursue action in court.
Michigan	Michigan Office of Financial and Insurance Services Consumer Services/ Benefits Inquiry Section P.O. Box 30220 Lansing, MI 48909-7720 Voice: 877-999-6442 Fax: 517-241-4168	Within 60 days after receiving notice of a final adverse determination by the insurer's internal review process, the enrollee may make a request to the commissioner for state review, who appoints an independent review organization if warranted.	Binding on the insurer. Enrollee may still take matter to court.
Minnesota	Ombudsman State Managed Health Care Program 444 Lafayette Road North St. Paul, MN 55155-3854 Voice: 651-296-1256 Fax: 651-282-6499	Enrollee may appeal a final adverse determination for any reason.	Binding only on the insurer. Insurer may seek judicial review of decision on grounds that it was arbitrary and capricious or involved an abuse of discretion.
Mississippi	*no state review board provided	—	—

State	Name, Address, and Phone Number of Regulating Agency	When Review Is Provided	Binding on Whom?
Missouri	Director of the Department of Insurance Consumer Services Division P.O. Box 690 Jefferson City, MO 65102 Voice: 800-726-7390 Fax: 573-526-4898	After adverse determination by health care provider based on medical necessity, appropriateness, health care setting, level of care, or effectiveness, enrollee may request state review.	Binding on the insurer and the enrollee.
Montana	Montana Department of Public Health and Human Services (department establishes a process for selecting peers to review adverse determinations by insurers) 111 North Sanders P.O. Box 4210 Helena, MT 59604-4210 Voice: 406-444-5622 Fax: 406-444-1970	Enrollee may appeal an adverse determination based on medical necessity or inappropriateness. The review is conducted by, and a decision is made by, a "peer," who is defined as another health care provider.	Binding on the insurer only.
Nebraska	Nebraska Department of Insurance Terminal Building 941 O Street, Suite 400 Lincoln, NE 68508-3639 Voice: 402-471-2201	Although there is no statute that provides for a state independent review, the Nebraska Department of Insurance has enacted its own regulations that allow an enrollee to appeal a health insurer's adverse determinations.	Binding on the insurer.
Nevada	*no state review board provided	—	—

State	Name, Address, and Phone Number of Regulating Agency	When Review Is Provided	Binding on Whom?
New Hampshire	New Hampshire Insurance Department (insurance commissioner certifies the independent review organizations) 56 Old Suncook Road Concord, NH 03301-7317 Voice: 603-271-2261 Fax: 603-271-1406	Within 180 days after final adverse determination of health care coverage (or if provider agrees to submit to review before that time) based on medical necessity, appropriateness, health care, setting, level of care, or effectiveness, an enrollee may request state review.	Binding on the insurer. Binding on the enrollee "except to the extent the covered person has other remedies available under federal or state law."
New Jersey	Commissioner of Health and Senior Services. (commissioner contracts with one or more independent review organizations to conduct reviews) Office of Managed Care of New Jersey P.O. Box 360, Room 604 Trenton, NJ 08625 Voice: 609-633-0660	Within 60 days after final adverse determination by health carrier based on medical necessity or appropriateness of services, enrollee may request state review in the Independent Health Care Appeals Program.	Decision is binding on the insurer, nonbinding on enrollee.
New Mexico	*no state review board provided	—	—
New York	New York State Insurance Department (superintendent of insurance has the power to grant and revoke certifications of state appeal agents) Empire State Plaza Agency Building #1 Albany, NY 12257 Voice: 800-400-8882	Within 45 days after a final adverse determination that a procedure is not medically necessary or is experimental or investigational, enrollee may request a state appeal conducted by "clinical peer reviewers."	Binding on the insurer *and* the enrollee.

State	Name, Address, and Phone Number of Regulating Agency	When Review Is Provided	Binding on Whom?
North Carolina	*no state review board provided	—	—
North Dakota	*no state review board provided	—	—
Ohio	State of Ohio Department of Insurance (superintendent of insurance is responsible for assigning independent review organizations) 2100 Stella Court Columbus, OH 43215 Attn: Managed Care Division Voice: 800-686-1526	Within 60 days after final adverse determination by insurer's internal appeals process, enrollee may request state review of a denial based on medical necessity.	Binding on the insurer.
Oklahoma	Oklahoma State Dept. of Health (certifies independent review organizations) 1000 Northeast 10th Street Oklahoma City, OK 73117 Voice: 405-271-5600	Within 30 days after denial based on an insurer's decision that the requested service or treatment is not medically necessary, appropriate, or effective, enrollee may request state review.	Decisions are *advisory* only. The state's HMOs, however, are apparently complying voluntarily.
Oregon	*no state review board provided	—	—
Pennsylvania	Pennsylvania Department of Health (assigns the independent review organizations) P.O. Box 90 Health & Welfare Bldg. Harrisburg, PA 17108 Voice: 877-PA-HEALTH	Within 15 days after exhaustion of insurer's internal appeals process, enrollee may request state review of decision to deny based on medical necessity or inappropriateness.	Binding on the insurer, but within 60 days after decision, either party may appeal in court. There is a rebuttable presumption in favor of the decision.

State	Name, Address, and Phone Number of Regulating Agency	When Review Is Provided	Binding on Whom?
Rhode Island	Rhode Island Department of Health (director of health promulgates rules and regulations pertaining to state appeal agencies) Managed Care Division 3 Capitol Hill, Room 410 Providence, RI 02908 Voice: 401-222-6015 Fax: 401-222-3017	Within 60 days after enrollee has exhausted an insurer's internal appeals process, the enrollee may request review of denial based on medical necessity.	Binding on the insurer. Enrollee may seek judicial review of adverse decision made by the state appeals agency.
South Carolina	Director of the South Carolina Department of Insurance P.O. Box 100105 Columbia, SC 29202-3105 Voice: 803-737-6180	Within 60 days after final adverse determination of coverage based on medical necessity, appropriateness, health care setting, level of care, or effectiveness, enrollee may make a written request to the health care provider for state review.	Binding on the insurer and on the enrollee "except to the extent the covered person has other remedies available under applicable federal or state law."
South Dakota	*no state review board provided	—	—
Tennessee	*no state review board provided	—	—
Texas	Texas Department of Insurance (commissioner of insurance promulgates rules and standards) P.O. Box 149104 Austin, TX 78714-9104 Department Main: 800-252-3439 Direct line: 512-322-4357	Enrollees may appeal a final adverse determination based on medical necessity and appropriateness. There is no time limit for filing an appeal, though the department asks that enrollees file appeals as soon as possible.	Binding on the insurer.

State	Name, Address, and Phone Number of Regulating Agency	When Review Is Provided	Binding on Whom?
Utah	Utah Insurance Department State Office Building, Room 3110 Salt Lake City, UT 84114 Voice: 801-538-3873.	Law gives the department the authority to promulgate rules and regulations regarding IRO review of health care decisions. Law is being formulated.	—
Vermont	Vermont Health Care Administration External Review Program 89 Main Street, 3rd Floor Drawer 20 Montpelier, VT 05620 Voice: 802-828-2900	Within 90 days of exhaustion of internal appeals process, enrollee may request review of adverse determination based on medical necessity, appropriateness, health care setting, level of care, or effectiveness.	Binding on the insurer.
Virginia	Bureau of Insurance, Office of the Managed Care Ombudsman 6th Floor P.O. Box 1157, Richmond, VA 23218 Voice: 804-371-9913 Fax: 804-371-9873	Within 30 days after a final adverse health decision made by insurer, enrollee may request state independent review by an "impartial health entity." The entity makes recommendations to the commissioner of insurance.	Commissioner determines whether to follow entity's recommendations. The final decision of the commissioner is binding on the insurer and enrollee and cannot be appealed.
Washington	State Department of Health 1112 SE Quince Street P.O. Box 47890 Olympia, WA 98504-7890 Voice: 360-236-4010	New law allows adverse determination based on medical necessity by insurer's internal process. Rules and regulations have yet to be promulgated by the department. Law is being formulated.	—

State	Name, Address, and Phone Number of Regulating Agency	When Review Is Provided	Binding on Whom?
West Virginia	*No state review board provided, although patients' bill of rights legislation is pending.	—	—
Wisconsin	*No state review board provision in place, although one is about to go into effect. The regulations regarding the independent review organizations, however, are not yet released.	—	—
Wyoming	*no state review board provided	—	—

Survey completed: March 2, 2001

Appendix C:
Insurance Commissions

ALABAMA

Alabama Department of Insurance
201 Monroe Street, Suite 1700
Montgomery, AL 36104
334-269-3550
Fax: 334-241-4192

ALASKA

Alaska Division of Insurance
3601 C Street, Suite 1324
Anchorage, AK 99503-5948
907-269-7900
Fax: 907-269-7912

Department of Community & Economic Development
P.O. Box 110805
Juneau, AK 99811-0805
907-465-2515
Fax: 907-465-3422
Use Anchorage as primary mailing address

ARIZONA

Arizona Department of Insurance
2910 North 44th Street, Suite 210
Phoenix, AZ 85018-7256
602-912-8400
Fax: 602-912-8452

ARKANSAS

Arkansas Department of Insurance
1200 West 3rd Street
Little Rock, AR 72201-1904
501-371-2600
Fax: 501-371-2629

CALIFORNIA

California Department of Insurance
300 Capitol Mall, Suite 1500
Sacramento, CA 95814
916-492-3500
Fax: 916-445-5280
or
45 Fremont Street, 23rd Floor
San Francisco, CA 94102
415-538-4040
Fax: 415-904-5889
or
300 South Spring Street
Los Angeles, CA 90013
213-346-6400
Fax: 213-897-6771

COLORADO

Colorado Division of Insurance
1560 Broadway, Suite 850
Denver, CO 80202
303-894-7499
Fax: 303-894-7455

Connecticut Department of Insurance
P.O. Box 816
Hartford, CT 06142-0816
860-297-3800
Fax: 860-566-7410

Federal Express packages:
153 Market Street, 11th Floor
Hartford, CT 06103

Delaware Department of Insurance
Rodney Building
841 Silver Lake Boulevard
Dover, DE 19904
302-739-4251
Fax: 302-739-5280

Department of Insurance and Securities Regulation
Government of the District of Columbia
810 First Street, NE, Suite 701
Washington, DC 20002
202-727-8000, ext. 3018
Fax: 202-535-1196

Florida Department of Insurance
State Capitol
Plaza Level 11
Tallahassee, FL 32399-0300
850-413-2804
Fax: 850-413-2950

Georgia Department of Insurance
2 Martin Luther King Jr. Drive
Floyd Memorial Building
704 West Tower
Atlanta, GA 30334
404-656-2056
Fax: 404-657-7493

Hawaii Insurance Division
Department of Commerce and Consumer Affairs
250 South King Street, 5th Floor
Honolulu, HI 96813
808-586-2790
Fax: 808-586-2806

Post office box address:
P.O. Box 3614
Honolulu, HI 96811-3614

Idaho Department of Insurance
700 West State Street, 3rd Floor
Boise, ID 83720-0043
208-334-4250
Fax: 208-334-4398

Illinois Department of Insurance
320 West Washington Street, 4th Floor
Springfield, IL 62767-0001
217-782-4515
Fax: 217-524-6500
or
100 West Randolph Street
Suite 15-100
Chicago, IL 60601-3251
312-814-2420
Fax: 312-814-5435

Indiana Department of Insurance
311 West Washington Street, Suite 300
Indianapolis, IN 46204-2787
317-232-2385
Fax: 317-232-5251

Division of Insurance
State of Iowa
330 East Maple Street
Des Moines, IA 50319
515-281-5705
Fax: 515-281-3059

Kansas Department of Insurance
420 SW 9th Street
Topeka, KS 66612-1678
785-296-7801
Fax: 785-296-2283

Kentucky Department of Insurance
P.O. Box 517
215 West Main Street
Frankfort, KY 40602-0517
502-564-6027
Fax: 502-564-1453

Louisiana Department of Insurance
950 North 5th Street
Baton Rouge, LA 70802
225-342-5423
Fax: 225-342-8622

Post office box address:
P.O. Box 94214
Baton Rouge, LA 70804-9214

Maine Bureau of Insurance
Department of Professional
and Financial Regulation
State Office Building, Station 34
Augusta, ME 04333-0034
207-624-8475
Fax: 207-624-8599

Federal Express packages:
124 Northern Avenue
Gardiner, ME 04345

Maryland Insurance Administration
525 St. Paul Place
Baltimore, MD 21202-2272
410-468-2090
Fax: 410-468-2020

Division of Insurance
Commonwealth of Massachusetts
One South Station, 4th Floor
Boston, MA 02110
617-521-7301
Fax: 617-521-7758

Michigan Insurance Bureau
Office of Financial and Insurance
  Services
611 West Ottawa Street,
  2nd Floor North
Lansing, MI 48933-1020
517-335-3167
Fax: 517-335-4978

**Minnesota Department of
Commerce**
85 Seventh Place East, Suite 500
St. Paul, MN 55101-2198
651-296-6025
Fax: 651-282-2568

**Mississippi Insurance
Department**
501 N. West Street
Woolfolk State Office Building,
  10th Floor
Jackson, MS 39201
601-359-3569
Fax: 601-359-2474

Post office box address:
P.O. Box 79
Jackson, MS 39205

**Missouri Department of
Insurance**
301 West High Street, Suite 530
Jefferson City, MO 65101
573-751-4126
Fax: 573-751-1165

**Montana Department of
Insurance**
840 Helena Avenue
Helena, MT 59601
406-444-2040
Fax: 406-444 3497

**Nebraska Department of
Insurance**
Terminal Building, Suite 400
941 O Street
Lincoln, NE 68508
402-471-2201
Fax: 402-471-4610

Nevada Division of Insurance
788 Fairview Drive, Suite 300
Carson City, NV 89701-5753
775-687-4270
Fax: 775-687-3937

Department of Insurance
State of New Hampshire
56 Old Suncook Road
Concord, NH 03301
603-271-2261
Fax: 603-271-1406

**New Jersey Department of
Insurance**
20 West State Street, CN325
Trenton, NJ 08625
609-292-5360
Fax: 609-984-5273

New Mexico Department of Insurance
P.O. Drawer 1269
Santa Fe, NM 87504-1269
505-827-4601
Fax: 505-476-0326

Federal Express packages:
PERA Building
1120 Paseo de Peralta
Santa Fe, NM 87501

NEW YORK
New York Department of Insurance
25 Beaver Street
New York, NY 10004-2319
212-480-2289
Fax: 212-480-2310

Agency Building One
Empire State Plaza
Albany, NY 12257
518-474-6600
Fax: 518-473-6814

NORTH CAROLINA
North Carolina Department of Insurance
P.O. Box 26387
Raleigh, NC 27611
919-733-3058
Fax: 919-733-6495

Federal Express packages:
Dobbs Building
430 North Salisbury Street
Raleigh, NC 27603

NORTH DAKOTA
North Dakota Department of Insurance
600 East Boulevard
Bismarck, ND 58505-0320
701-328-2440
Fax: 701-328-4880

OHIO
Ohio Department of Insurance
2100 Stella Court
Columbus, OH 43215-1067
614-644-2658
Fax: 614-644-3743

OKLAHOMA
Oklahoma Department of Insurance
2401 NW 23rd Street, Suite 28
Oklahoma City, OK 73107
405-521-2828
Fax: 405-521-6635

OREGON
Oregon Insurance Division
350 Winter Street NE, Room 440
Salem, OR 97310-3883
503-947-7980
Fax: 503-378-4351

PENNSYLVANIA
Pennsylvania Insurance Department
1326 Strawberry Square, 13th Floor
Harrisburg, PA 17120
717-783-0442
Fax: 717-772-1969

Rhode Island Insurance Division
Department of Business
 Regulation
233 Richmond Street, Suite 233
Providence, RI 02903-4233
401-222-2223
Fax: 401-222-5475

South Carolina Department of Insurance
1612 Marion Street
Columbia, SC 29201
803-737-6160
Fax: 803-737-6229

Post office box address:
P.O. Box 100105
Columbia, SC 29202-3105

South Dakota Division of Insurance
Department of Commerce and
 Regulation
118 West Capitol Avenue
Pierre, SD 57501-2000
605-773-3563
Fax: 605-773-5369

Tennessee Department of Commerce and Insurance
Volunteer Plaza
500 James Robertson Parkway
Nashville, TN 37243-0565
615-741-2241
Fax: 615-532-6934

Texas Department of Insurance
333 Guadalupe Street
Austin, TX 78701
512-463-6464
Fax: 512-475-2005

Post office box address:
P.O. Box 149104
Austin, TX 78714-9104

Utah Department of Insurance
3110 State Office Building
Salt Lake City, UT 84114-1201
801-538-3800
Fax: 801-538-3829

Vermont Division of Insurance
Department of Banking,
 Insurance and Securities
89 Main Street, Drawer 20
Montpelier, VT 05620-3101
802-828-3301
Fax: 802-828-3306

State Corporation Commission
Bureau of Insurance
Commonwealth of Virginia
P.O. Box 1157
Richmond, VA 23218
804-371-9694
Fax: 804-371-9873

Washington Office of the Insurance Commissioner
14th Avenue and Water Street
P.O. Box 40255
Olympia, WA 98504-0255
360-664-8137
Fax: 360-586-3535

WEST VIRGINIA

West Virginia Department of Insurance
P.O. Box 50540
Charleston, WV 25305-0540
304-558-3354
Fax: 304-558-0412

Federal Express packages:
State of West Virginia
1124 Smith Street
Charleston, WV 25301

WISCONSIN

Office of the Commissioner of Insurance
121 East Wilson
Madison, WI 53702
608-267-1233
Fax: 608-261-8579

Post office box address:
P.O. Box 7873
Madison, WI 53707-7873

WYOMING

Wyoming Department of Insurance
Herschler Building
122 West 25th Street,
    3rd Floor East
Cheyenne, WY 82002-0440
307-777-7401
Fax: 307-777-5895

Appendix C:
Banking Agencies

ALABAMA

Superintendent of Banks
Center for Commerce
401 Adams Avenue, #680
Montgomery, AL 36130-1201
334-242-3452
Fax: 334-242-3500
Web site: www.legislature.
    state.al.us

ALASKA

Director of Banking
Securities and Corporations
Department of Commerce
P.O. Box 110807
150 Third Street, Room 217
Juneau, AK 99811-0807
907-465-2521
TDD: 907-465-5437
Fax: 907-465-2549
E-mail: dbsc@dced.state.ak.us
Web site: www.dced.state.ak.us

ARIZONA

Superintendent of Banks
Arizona State Banking
Department
2910 North 44th Street, Suite 310
Phoenix, AZ 85018
602-255-4421
Toll free in AZ: 800-544-0708
Fax: 602-381-1225
Web site: www.azbanking.com

ARKANSAS

Bank Commissioner
Arkansas State Bank
Department
Tower Building
323 Center Street, Suite 500
Little Rock, AR 72201-2613
501-324-9019
Fax: 501-324-9028
E-mail: asbdbanking.state.ar.us
Web site: www.state.ar.us/bank

CALIFORNIA

Commissioner
Department of Financial
Institutions
State of California
111 Pine Street, Suite 1100
San Francisco, CA 94111-5613
415-263-8507
Toll free in CA: 800-622-0620
Fax: 415-989-5310
E-mail: consumer@dfi.ca.gov
Web site: www.dfi.ca.gov

COLORADO

State Bank Commissioner
Department of Regulatory
    Agencies
Division of Banking
1560 Broadway, Suite 1175
Denver, CO 80202
303-894-7575
Fax: 303-894-7570
E-mail: banking@dora.state.co.us
Web site: www.dora.state.co.us/
    banking

Banking Commissioner
Connecticut Department of
Banking
260 Constitution Plaza
Hartford, CT 06103
860-240-8200
Toll free in CT: 800-831-7225
Fax: 860-240-8178
E-mail: john.burke@po.state.ct.us
Web site: www.state.ct.us/dob

State Bank Commissioner
Delaware Office of State Bank
Commissioner
555 East Lockerman Street,
   Suite 210
Dover, DE 19901
302-739-4235
Fax: 302-739-3609
Web site: www.state.de.us/bank

Commissioner of Banking and
Financial Institutions
Office of Banking and Finance
1400 L Street, NW
Washington, DC 20005
202-727-1563
Fax: 202-727-1588
Web site: www.obfi.dcgov.org

State Comptroller
Department of Banking and
Finance
101 East Gaines Street
Tallahassee, FL 32399-0350
850-410-9370
850-410-9275 (investigations)
Toll free in FL: 800-848-3792
Fax: 850-410-9026
E-mail: dbf@mail.dbf.state.fl.us
Web site: www.dbf.state.fl.us

Legal and Consumer Affairs
Specialist
State of Georgia (Department
of Banking and Finance)
2990 Brandywine Road, Suite 200
Atlanta, GA 30341-5565
770-986-1633
E-mail: neville@dbf.state.ga.us

Commissioner
Financial Institutions
State of Hawaii
P.O. Box 2054
1010 Richards Street, Room 602A
Honolulu, HI 96805
808-586-2820
Toll free in Kauai: 800-274-3141
Toll free in Maui: 800-984-2400
Toll free in Hawaii: 800-974-4000
   808-586-2820
Fax: 808-586-2818

Director
State of Idaho Department
of Finance
700 West State Street, 2nd Floor
Boise, ID 83720-0031
208-332-8000
Toll free in ID: 888-346-3376
Fax: 208-332-8098
E-mail: finance@fin.state.id.us
Web site: www.state.id.us/
  finance/dof.htm

Commissioner of Banks and
Real Estate
Illinois Office of Banks and
Real Estate
310 South Michigan Avenue,
  Suite 230
Chicago, IL 60604-4278
312-793-3000
Toll free: 877-793-3470
TDD/TTY: 312-793-0291
Fax: 312-793-0291
Web site: www.state.il.us/obr

Illinois Office of Banks and
Real Estate
Springfield Office
500 East Monroe Street
Springfield, IL 62701-1509
217-782-3000
TDD/TTY: 217-524-6644
Fax: 217-524-5941
Web site: www.state.il.us/obr

Director
Department of Financial
Institutions
402 West Washington Street,
  Room W-066
Indianapolis, IN 46204-2759
317-232-3955
Toll free in IN: 800-382-4880
Fax: 317-232-7655
E-mail: cphillips@dfi.state.in.us
Web site: www.dfi.state.in.us

Superintendent of Banking
Iowa Division of Banking
200 East Grand, Suite 300
Des Moines, IA 50309
515-281-4014
Toll free nationwide: 800-972-2018
Fax: 515-281-4862
E-mail: idob@max.state.ia.us
Web site: www.idob.state.ia.us

State Bank Commissioner
Office of the State Bank
  Commissioner
700 Jackson Street, Suite 300
Topeka, KS 66603-3714
785-296-2266
Fax: 785-296-0168
Web site: www.ink.org/public/
  osbc

Commissioner
Department of Financial
Institutions
1025 Capitol Center Drive,
Suite 200
Frankfort, KY 40601
502-573-3390
Toll free: 800-223-2579
Fax: 502-573-8787
Web site: www.dfi.state.ky.us

Commissioner
Louisiana Office of Financial
Institutions
P.O. Box 94095
Baton Rouge, LA 70804-9095
225-925-4660
Fax: 225-925-4524
E-mail: la_ofi@mail.premier.net
Web site: www.ofi.state.la.us

Superintendent of Banking
36 State House Station
Augusta, ME 04333-0036
207-624-8570
Toll free: 800-985-5235
TDD: 207-624-8563
Fax: 207-624-8590
Web site:
www.mainebankingreg.org

Commissioner of Financial
Regulation Division
500 North Calvert Street
Baltimore, MD 21202
410-333-6808
Toll free in MD: 888-784-0136
TTY: 410-767-2117
Fax: 410-333-0475
E-mail: fin_reg@dllr.state.md.us
Web site: www.dllr.state.md.us/
finance

Commissioner of Banks
Massachusetts Division
of Banks
One South Station
Boston, MA 02110
617-956-1500
Toll free in MA: 800-495-2265
TDD: 617-956-1577
Fax: 617-956-1597
Web site: www.state.ma.us/dob

Commissioner
Financial Institutions Bureau
Office of the Commissioner
333 South Capitol Avenue,
Suite A
P.O. Box 30224 (48909)
Lansing, MI 48933
517-373-3460
Fax: 517-335-1109
Web site: www.cis.state.mi.us/fib

Assistant Commissioner
Minnesota Department of
Commerce
Financial Exams
133 East Seventh Street
St. Paul, MN 55101
651-296-2751
Fax: 651-296-8591
E-mail:
   kevin.murphy@state.mn.us
Web site: www.commerce.
   state.mn.us

Director Consumer Finance
Division
Department of Banking and
Consumer Finance
P.O. Box 23729
550 High Street
Suite 304, Walter Sillers Building
Jackson, MS 39205-3729
601-359-1031
Toll free in MS: 800-844-2499
Fax: 601-359-3557
E-mail: tbrady@dbcf@state.ms.us
Web site: www.dbcf.state.ms.us

Acting Commissioner of
Finance
Department of Finance
P.O. Box 716
Jefferson City, MO 65102
573-751-3242
Toll free in MO: 800-735-2966
TDD toll free in MO: 800-735-2966
Fax: 573-751-9192
E-mail: finance@mail.state.mo.us
Web site: www.ecodev.state.
   mo.us/finance

Commissioner
Division of Banking and
Financial Institutions
846 Front Street
P.O. Box 200546
Helena, MT 59620-0546
406-444-2091
Fax: 406-444-4186
Web site:
   www.commerce.state.mt.us/
   finance/index.html

Director
Department of Banking
and Finance
1200 N Street, Suite 311
P.O. Box 95006
Lincoln, NE 68509
402-471-2171
Fax: 402-471-3062
Web site: www.ndbf.org

Commissioner
Department of Business and
Industry
Financial Institutions Division
406 East Second Street, Suite 3
Carson City, NV 89701-4758
775-687-4259
Toll free in NV: 800-521-0019
Fax: 775-687-6909
E-mail: swalshaw@govmail-
   state.nv.us
Web site: www.state.nv.us/b&i

**State of New Hampshire
Banking Department
Consumer Credit**
56 Old Suncook Road
Concord, NH 03301
603-271-3561
TTY/TDD: 800-735-2964
Fax: 603-271-1090
Web site: www.state.nh.us/
banking

**Acting Commissioner
Department of Banking and
Insurance**
20 West State Street
P.O. Box 325
Trenton, NJ 08625
609-292-3420
Fax: 609-984-5273
Web site: states.naic.org/nj/
njhomepg.html

**Financial Institutions Division
Regulation and Licensing
Department**
P.O. Box 25101
725 St. Michaels Drive
Santa Fe, NM 87501
505-827-7100
Fax: 505-827-7107
E-mail: rld@state.nm.us
Web site: www.state.nm.us

**Superintendent of Banking
New York State Banking
Department**
Two Rector Street
New York, NY 10006-1894
212-618-6553
Toll free in NY: 800-522-3330
(consumer services hotline)
Toll free in NY: 800-832-1838
(small business information)
Fax: 212-618-6599
Web site: www.banking.state.
ny.us

**North Carolina Commissioner
of Banks**
4309 Mail Service Center
Raleigh, NC 27699-4309
919-733-3016
Fax: 919-733-6918
Web site: www.banking.state.
nc.us

**Commissioner, North Dakota
Department of Banking and
Financial Institutions**
2000 Schafer Street, Suite G
Bismarck, ND 58501-1204
701-328-9933
TDD toll free in ND: 800-366-6888
Fax: 701-328-9955
E-mail: banking@state.nd.us
Web site: www.state.nd.us/bank

Training and Communications Manager
Department of Commerce, State of Ohio
Financial Institutions Division
77 South High Street, 21st Floor
Columbus, OH 43266-0121
614-728-8400
614-466-2932
Fax: 614-644-1631
Web site: www.som.state.oh.us/
   dfi

Bank Commissioner
Oklahoma State Banking Department
4545 North Lincoln Boulevard,
   Suite 164
Oklahoma City, OK 73105
405-521-2782
Fax: 405-522-2993
Web site: www.state.ok.us/~osbd

Administrator
Department of Consumer and Business Services
Division of Finance and Corporate
350 Winter Street, NE, Room 410
Salem, OR 97310-3881
503-378-4140
TDD: 503-378-4387
Fax: 503-947-7862
Web site: www.cbs.state.or.us/
   external/dfcs

Secretary of Banking Department
333 Market Street, 16th Floor
Harrisburg, PA 17101-2290
717-787-6991
Toll free in PA: 800-PA-BANKS
TDD toll free: 800-679-5070
Fax: 717-787-8773
Web site: www.banking.state.
   pa.us

Associate Director and Superintendent, Banking
233 Richmond Street, Suite 231
Providence, RI 02903-4231
401-222-2405
401-222-2999
Fax: 401-222-5628

Commissioner of Banking
State Board of Financial
   Institutions
1015 Sumter Street, Room 309
Columbia, SC 29201
803-734-2001
Fax: 803-734-2013

Director
South Dakota Division of Banking
217½ West Missouri Avenue
Pierre, SD 57501-4590
605-773-3421
Fax: 605-773-5367
Web site: www.state.sd.us/
   banking

Commissioner
Tennessee Department of
Financial Institutions
John Sevier Building
500 Charlotte Avenue, 4th Floor
Nashville, TN 37243-0705
615-741-2236
Fax: 615-741-2883
E-mail: tsmith@mail.state.tn.us
Web site: www.state.tn.us/
financialinst

Banking Commissioner
Texas Department of Banking
2601 North Lamar
Austin, TX 78705
512-475-1300
Toll free in TX: 877-276-5554
Fax: 512-475-1313
Web site: www.banking.state.
tx.us

Commissioner
Department of Financial
Institutions
P.O. Box 89
Salt Lake City, UT
84110-0089
801-538-8854
Fax: 801-538-8894
Web site: www.dfi.state.ut.us

Information Policy & Program
Chief
State of Vermont
Banking, Insurance, Securities
and Health Care
Administration
89 Main Street, Drawer 20
Montpelier, VT 05620-3101
802-828-4872
802-828-3307 (banking)
Toll free: 800-964-1764 (all
insurance except health)
Toll free: 800-631-7788 (health
care)
Fax: 802-828-3306
E-mail: rdaily@bishca.state.vt.us
Web site: www.state.vt.us/bis

Commissioner
Bureau of Financial
Institutions
1300 East Main Street, Suite 800
P.O. Box 640
Richmond, VA 23218-0640
804-371-9657
Toll free in VA: 800-552-7945
TDD: 804-371-9206
Fax: 804-371-9416
Web site: www.state.va.us/scc

Director
Department of Financial
Institutions
P.O. Box 41200
Olympia, WA 98504-1200
360-902-8707
Toll free: 800-372-8303
Fax: 360-586-5068
Web site: www.wa.gov/dfi

Commissioner
State Capitol Complex
Division of Banking
Building 3, Room 311
1900 Kanawha Boulevard East
Charleston, WV 25305-0240
304-558-2294
Toll free in WV: 800-642-9056
Fax: 304-558-0442
Web site: www.wvdob.org

Secretary
Department of Financial
Institutions
345 West Washington Avenue,
    5th Floor
P.O. Box 7876
Madison, WI 53708-8861
608-261-1622
Toll free in WI: 800-452-3328
Fax: 608-264-7968
Web site: www.wdfi.org

Commissioner
Division of Banking
Herschler Building, 3rd Floor East
Cheyenne, WY 82002
307-777-7797
Fax: 307-777-3555
E-mail: banking@state.wy.us
Web site: audit.state.wy.us/
    banking/default.htm

Appendix C:
Education Agencies

Alabama Department of Education
Gordon Persons Office Building
50 North Ripley Street
P.O. Box 302102
Montgomery, AL 36130-2101
334-242-9700
Fax: 334-242-9708
E-mail: dmurray@
  sdenet.alsde.edu
Web site: www.alsde.edu

ALASKA
Alaska Department of Education and Early Development
801 West 10th Street, Suite 200
Juneau, AK 99801-1894
907-465-2800
TTY: 907-465-2800
Fax: 907-465-4156
Web site: www.eed.state.ak.us

ARIZONA
Arizona Department of Education
1535 West Jefferson
Phoenix, AZ 85007
602-542-5460
Fax: 602-542-5440
E-mail: lkeegan@
  mail1.ade.state.az.us
Web site: www.ade.state.az.us

ARKANSAS
Arkansas Department of Education
General Education Division
Four State Capitol Mall,
  Room 304-A
Little Rock, AR 72201-1071
501-682-4204
Fax: 501-682-1079
E-mail: rsimon@arkedu.k12.ar.us
Web site: arkedu.state.ar.us

CALIFORNIA
California Department of Education
721 Capitol Mall, Second Floor
Sacramento, CA 95814
916-657-2451
Fax: 916-657-2682
E-mail: jcummings@cde.ca.gov
Web site: www.cde.ca.gov

COLORADO
Colorado Department of Education
201 East Colfax Avenue
Denver, CO 80203-1704
303-866-6600
Fax: 303-830-0793
E-mail: Howerter_C@
  cde.state.co.us
Web site: www.cde.state.co.us

Connecticut Department of Education
State Office Building, Room 305
165 Capitol Avenue
Hartford, CT 06106-1080
860-566-5061
Fax: 860-566-8964
E-mail: thomas.murphy@po.state.
  ct.us
Web site: www.state.ct.us/sde

Delaware Department of Education
John G. Townsend Building
Federal and Lockerman Streets
P.O. Box 1402
Dover, DE 19903-1402
302-739-4601
Fax: 302-739-4654
Web site: www.doe.state.de.us

District of Columbia Public Schools
Union Square
825 North Capitol Street, NE
Washington, DC 20002
202-724-4222
Fax: 202-442-5026
Web site: www.k12.dc.us

Florida Department of Education
Capitol Building, Room PL 08
Tallahassee, FL 32399-0400
850-487-1785
Fax: 850-413-0378
Web site: www.firn.edu/
  doe/index.html

Georgia Department of Education
2054 Twin Towers East
205 Butler Street
Atlanta, GA 30334-5001
404-656-2800
Toll free in GA: 800-311-3627
Fax: 404-651-6867
E-mail: state.superintendent@
  doe.k12.ga.us
Web site: www.doe.k12.ga.us/
  index.asp

Hawaii Department of Education
1390 Miller Street
Honolulu, HI 96813
808-586-3310
Fax: 808-586-3320
E-mail: supt_doe@notes.k12.hi.us
Web site: www.k12.hi.us

Idaho Department of Education
Len B. Jordan Office Building
650 West State Street
P.O. Box 83720
Boise, ID 83720-0027
208-332-6800
Toll free in ID: 800-432-4601
TTY: 800-377-3529
Fax: 208-334-2228
Web site: www.sde.state.id.
  us/Dept

Illinois State Board of Education

100 North First Street
Springfield, IL 62777
217-782-4321
TTY: 217-782-1900
Fax: 217-524-4928
E-mail: gmcgee@
  smtt.isbe.state.il.us
Web site: www.isbe.state.il.us/

Indiana Department of Education

State House, Room 229
Indianapolis, IN 46204-2798
317-232-6665
Fax: 317-232-8004
Web site: www.doe.state.in.us

Iowa Department of Education

Grimes State Office Building
East 14th and Grand Streets
Des Moines, IA 50319-0146
515-281-3436
Fax: 515-281-4122
E-mail: ted.stilwill@ed.state.ia.us
Web site: www.state.ia.us/educate

Kansas Department of Education

120 SE 10th Avenue
Topeka, KS 66612-1182
785-296-3201
Fax: 785-296-7933
E-mail: atompkins@
  ksbe.state.ks.us
  or
  lasnider@ksbe.state.ks.us
Web site: www.ksbe.state.ks.us

Kentucky Department of Education

500 Mero Street
Frankfort, KY 40601
502-564-4770
Toll free in KY: 800-533-5372
Fax: 502-564-6470
E-mail: kwilborn@kde.state.ky.us
Web site: www.kde.state.ky.us

Louisiana Department of Education

626 North Fourth Street
P.O. Box 94064
Baton Rouge, LA 70704-9064
225-342-4411
Fax: 225-342-7316
E-mail: webmaster@
  mail.doe.state.la.us
Web site: www.doe.state.la.us

Maine Department of Education

23 State House Station
Augusta, ME 04333-0023
207-287-5800
TTY: 207-287-2550
Fax: 207-287-5802
Web site: janus.state.me.us/
  education/homepage.htm

Maryland Department of Education

200 West Baltimore Street
Baltimore, MD 21201
410-767-0462
Fax: 410-333-6033
Web site: www.msde.state.md.us

Massachusetts Department of Education
Educational Improvement Group
350 Main Street
Malden, MA 02148
781-338-3000
TTY: 800-439-2370
Fax: 781-338-3392
E-mail: www@doe.mass.edu
Web site: www.doe.mass.edu

MICHIGAN
Michigan Department of Education
Hannah Building, 4th Floor
608 West Allegan Street
Lansing, MI 48933
517-373-3324
Fax: 517-335-4565
Web site: www.mde.state.mi.us

MINNESOTA
Minnesota Department of Children, Families, and Learning
1500 Highway 36 West
Roseville, MN 55113-4266
651-582-8200
TTY: 651-582-8201
Fax: 651-582-8202
E-mail: children@state.mn.us
Web site: cfl.state.mn.us

MISSISSIPPI
Mississippi State Department of Education
359 North West Street, Suite 365
Jackson, MS 39201
601-359-3513
Fax: 601-359-3242
Web site: www.mde.k12.ms.us

MISSOURI
Missouri Department of Elementary and Secondary Education
P.O. Box 480
Jefferson City, MO 65102-0480
573-751-4212
TTY: 800-735-2966
Fax: 573-751-8613
E-mail: pubinfo@
    mail.dese.state.mo.us
Web site: www.dese.state.mo.us

MONTANA
Montana Office of Public Instruction
P.O. Box 202501
Helena, MT 59620-2501
406-444-2082
Fax: 406-444-3924
E-mail: cbergeron@state.mt.us
Web site: www.metnet.state.mt.us

NEBRASKA
Nebraska Department of Education
301 Centennial Mall South
P.O. Box 94987
Lincoln, NE 68509-4987
402-471-2295
TTY: 402-471-7295
Fax: 402-471-0017
E-mail: eduneb@nde.state.ne.us
Web site: www.nde.state.ne.us

Nevada State Department of Education
700 East Fifth Street
Carson City, NV 89701
775-687-9141
Fax: 775-687-9101
E-mail: fsouth@nsn.K12.nv.us
Web site: www.nsn.k12.nv.us/
nvdoe

New Hampshire Department of Education
101 Pleasant Street
State Office Park South
Concord, NH 03301
603-271-3144
800-339-9900
TTY: 800-735-2964
Fax: 603-271-1953
E-mail: llovering@ed.state.nh.us
Web site: www.ed.state.nh.us

New Jersey Department of Education
P.O. Box 500
100 Riverview Place
Trenton, NJ 08625-0500
609-292-4469
Fax: 609-777-4099
Web site: www.state.nj.us/
education

New Mexico State Department of Education
Education Building
300 Don Gaspar
Santa Fe, NM 87501-2786
505-827-6516
TTY: 505-827-6541
Fax: 505-827-6696
Web site: sde.state.nm.us

New York Education Department
Education Building
89 Washington Avenue, Room 111
Albany, NY 12234
518-474-5844
Fax: 518-473-4909
E-mail: rmills@mail.nysed.gov
Web site: www.nysed.gov

North Carolina Department of Public Instruction
Education Building
301 North Wilmington Street
Raleigh, NC 27601-2825
919-715-1299
Fax: 919-715-1278
Web site:
www.ncpublicschools.org

North Dakota Department of Public Instruction
11th Floor, Department 201
600 East Boulevard Avenue
Bismarck, ND 58505-0440
701-328-2260
Fax: 701-328-2461
E-mail: wsanstea@
  mail.dpi.state.nd.us
  or
  tlalonde@mail.dpi.state.nd.us
Web site: www.dpi.state.nd.us

Ohio Department of Education
65 South Front Street, Room 1005
Columbus, OH 43215-4183
877-644-6338
Fax: 614-644-5960
E-mail: ims_help@ode.state.oh.us
Web site: www.ode.state.oh.us

Oklahoma State Department of Education
2500 North Lincoln Boulevard
Oklahoma City, OK 73105-4599
405-521-3301
Fax: 405-521-6205
E-mail: sandy_garrett@
  mail.sde.state.ok.us
Web site: sde.state.ok.us

Oregon Department of Education
255 Capitol Street, NE
Salem, OR 97310-0203
503-378-3569
TTY: 503-378-2892
Fax: 503-373-7968
E-mail: larry.austin@state.or.us
Web site: www.ode.state.or.us

Pennsylvania Department of Education
333 Market Street, 10th Floor
Harrisburg, PA 17126-0333
717-787-5820
Fax: 717-787-7222
E-mail: sec@state.psu.edu
Web site: www.pde.psu.edu

Rhode Island Department of Elementary and Secondary Education
255 Westminster Street
Providence, RI 02903-3400
401-222-4600
TTY: 800-745-5555
Fax: 401-222-4044
E-mail: ride0015@ride.ri.net
Web site: www.ridoe.net

South Carolina Department of Education
1006 Rutledge Building
1429 Senate Street
Columbia, SC 29201
803-734-8492
Fax: 803-734-3389
Web site: www.state.sc.us/sde/

South Dakota Department of Education and Cultural Affairs
700 Governors Drive
Pierre, SD 57501-2291
605-773-3134
TTY: 605-773-6302
Fax: 605-773-6139
E-mail: janelle.toman@state.sd.us
or
tamara.darnall@state.sd.us
Web site: www.state.sd.us/deca

Tennessee State Department of Education
Andrew Johnson Tower, 6th Floor
710 James Robertson Parkway
Nashville, TN 37243-0375
615-741-2731
Fax: 615-532-4791
E-mail: vcoffey@mail.state.tn.us
Web site: www.state.tn.us/
education

Texas Education Agency
William B. Travis Building
1701 North Congress Avenue
Austin, TX 78701-1494
512-463-9734
Fax: 512-463-9008
Web site: www.tea.state.tx.us

Utah State Office of Education
250 East 500 South
Salt Lake City, UT 84111
801-538-7500
Fax: 801-538-7521
E-mail: SLAING@usoe.k12.ut.us
Web site: www.usoe.k12.ut.us

Vermont Department of Education
120 State Street
Montpelier, VT 05620-2501
802-828-3147
TTY: 802-828-2755
Fax: 802-828-3140
E-mail: edinfo@doe.state.vt.us
Web site: www.state.vt.us/educ

Virginia Department of Education
P.O. Box 2120
101 North 14th Street
Richmond, VA 23218-2120
804-225-2020
Toll free in VA: 800-292-3820
Fax: 804-371-2455
E-mail: cmakela@pen.k12.va.us
Web site: www.pen.k12.va.us/
go/VDOE

Office of Superintendent of Public Instruction
Old Capitol Building
600 South Washington
P.O. Box 47200
Olympia, WA 98504-7200
360-586-6904
TTY: 360-664-3631
Fax: 360-753-6712
Web site: www.k12.wa.us

West Virginia Department of Education
Building 6
1900 Kanawha Boulevard East
Charleston, WV 25305-0330
304-558-0304
Fax: 304-558-2584
E-mail: wvde@access.k12.wv.us
Web site: wvde.state.wv.us

Wisconsin Department of Public Instruction
125 South Webster Street
P.O. Box 7841
Madison, WI 53707-7841
608-266-3108
800-441-4563
TTY: 608-267-2427
Fax: 608-267-1052
Web site: www.dpi.state.wi.us

Wyoming Department of Education
2300 Capitol Avenue, 2nd Floor
Cheyenne, WY 82002
307-777-7675
TTY: 307-777-6221
Fax: 307-777-6234
E-mail: jcatch@educ.state.wy.us
Web site: www.k12.wy.us

Appendix C:
Agencies That Accept Consumer Complaints Against Credit Card Companies

For all credit cards issued by a national bank*, contact:

Office of the Comptroller of Currency
1301 McKinney Street, Suite 3710
Houston, TX 77010
Fax: 713-336 4301

For all other credit cards, a complaint can be filed with either a state agency, if it accepts it, or with the FTC:

Federal Trade Commission
Consumer Response Center
CRC-240
600 Pennsylvania Avenue, NW
Washington, DC 20580
877-FTC-HELP (877-382-4357)

ALABAMA
Consumer Affairs Division
Office of the Attorney General
11 South Union Street
Montgomery, AL 36130
334-242-7334
Toll free in AL: 800-392-5658
Web site: www.ago.state.al.us

ALASKA
Consumer Protection Unit
Office of the Attorney General
1031 West 4th Avenue, Suite 200
Anchorage, AK 99501-5903
907-269-5100
Fax: 907-276-8554
Web site: www.law.state.ak.us

ARIZONA
OCC or FTC

ARKANSAS
Consumer Protection Division
Office of the Attorney General
323 Center Street, Suite 200
Little Rock, AR 72201
501-682-2341
Voice/TDD toll free in AR:
    800-482-8982
Toll free: 800-482-8982
TDD: 501-682-6073
Fax: 501-682-8118
E-mail: consumer@ag.state.ar.us
Web site: www.ag.state.ar.us

Note: In several states consumer complaints are to be directed to the federal agencies OCC or FTC, as listed here.

*National banks are chartered by the federal government and have the word "national" or carry the abbreviation "N.A." or "N.S.&T." in their name.

CALIFORNIA
Office of the Attorney General
Public Inquiry Unit
P.O. Box 944255
Sacramento, CA 94244-2550
916-322-3360
Toll free in CA: 800-952-5225
TDD: 916-324-5564
Web site: www.caag.state.ca.us/
piu

COLORADO
OCC or FTC

CONNECTICUT
Antitrust/Consumer Protection
Office of Attorney General
110 Sherman Street
Hartford, CT 06105
860-808-5400
Fax: 860-808-5593
Web site: www.cslnet.ctstateu.
edu/attygen

Department of Consumer
Protection
165 Capitol Avenue
Hartford, CT 06106
860-713-6050
Toll free in CT: 800-842-2649
Fax: 860-566-1531
Web site: www.state.ct.us/dcp

DELAWARE
Delaware Office of State Bank
Commissioner
555 East Lockerman Street,
Suite 210
Dover, DE 19901
302-739-4235
Fax: 302-739-3609
Web site: www.state.de.us/bank

DISTRICT OF COLUMBIA
Office of Banking & Financial
Institutions
1400 L Street, NW, Suite 400
Washington, DC 20005
202-727-1563
Fax: 202-727-1588

FLORIDA
Department of Agriculture
and Consumer Services
407 South Calhoun Street
Mayo Building, 2nd Floor
Tallahassee, FL 32399-0800
850-922-2966
Toll free in FL: 800-435-7352
Fax: 850-487-4177
Web site: www.fl-ag.com

GEORGIA
Governor's Office of
Consumer Affairs
2 Martin Luther King Jr. Drive,
Suite 356
Atlanta, GA 30334
404-651-8600
Toll free in GA outside Atlanta
area: 800-869-1123
Fax: 404-651-9018
Web site: www2.state.ga.us/
gaoca

HAWAII
Office of Consumer Protection
Department of Commerce and
Consumer Affairs
235 South Beretania Street,
Room 801
Honolulu, HI 96813
808-586-2636
Fax: 808-586-2640

Consumer Protection Unit
Idaho Attorney General's
Office
650 West State Street
Boise, ID 83720-0010
208-334-2424
Toll free in ID: 800-432-3545
Fax: 208-334-2830
Web site: www.state.id.us/ag

OCC or FTC

Consumer Protection Division
Office of the Attorney General
Indiana Government Center
    South
402 West Washington Street,
    5th Floor
Indianapolis, IN 46204
317-232-6330
Toll free in IN: 800-382-5516
Fax: 317-233-4393
E-mail: inattgn@atg.state.in.us
Web site: www.ai.org/
    hoosieradvocate

Consumer Protection Division
Office of the Attorney General
1300 East Walnut Street,
    2nd Floor
Des Moines, IA 50319
515-281-5926
Fax: 515-281-6771
E-mail: consumer@ag.state.ia.us
Web site: www.state.ia.us/
    government/ag/consumer.html

Consumer Protection Division
Office of the Attorney General
120 SW 10th, 4th Floor
Topeka, KS 66612-1597
785-296-3751
Toll free in KS: 800-432-2310
TDD/TTY: 785-291-3767
Fax: 785-291-3699
E-mail: cprotect@ksag.org
Web site: www.ink.org/public/
    ksag

Consumer Protection Division
Office of the Attorney General
1024 Capital Center Drive
Frankfort, KY 40601
502-696-5389
Toll free in KY: 888-432-9257
Fax: 502-573-8317
E-mail: attorney.general@
    law.state.ky.us
Web site: www.law.state.ky.us/cp

Consumer Protection Division
Office of the Attorney General
9001 Shelbyville Road, Suite 3
Louisville, KY 40222
502-425-4825
Fax: 502-425-9406

Consumer Protection Section
Office of the Attorney General
301 Main Street, Suite 1250
Baton Rouge, LA 70801
225-342-9639
Toll free: 800-351-4889
Fax: 225-342-9637
Web site: www.laag.com

Office of Consumer Credit Regulation
35 State House Station
Augusta, ME 04333-0035
207-624-8527
Toll free in ME: 800-332-8529
TDD/TTY: 207-624-8563
Web site:
www.mainecreditreg.org

Consumer Protection Division
Office of the Attorney General
200 Saint Paul Place, 16th Floor
Baltimore, MD 21202-2021
410-528-8662 (consumer
complaint hotline)
410-576-6550 (consumer
information)
TDD MD only: 410-576-06372
Fax: 410-576-7040
E-mail: consumer@
oag.state.md.us
Web site: www.oag.state.md.us/
consumer

Consumer Protection and
Antitrust Division
Office of the Attorney General
200 Portland Street
Boston, MA 02114
617-727-8400
Fax: 617-727-5765
Web site: www.ago.state.ma.us

Consumer Protection Division
Office of the Attorney General
P.O. Box 30213
Lansing, MI 48909
517-373-1140 (complaint
information)
517-373-1110
Fax: 517-335-1935

Consumer Services Division
Minnesota Attorney General's
Office
1400 NCL Tower
445 Minnesota Street
St. Paul, MN 55101
651-296-3353
Toll free: 800-657-3787
Fax: 612-282-5801
E-mail: consumer.ag@state.mn.us
Web site: www.ag.state.mn.us/
consumer

Consumer Protection Division
of the Mississippi Attorney
General's Office
P.O. Box 22947
Jackson, MS 39225-2947
601-359-4230
Toll free in MS: 800-281-4418
Fax: 601-359-4231
Web site: www.ago.state.ms.us/
consprot.htm

**Bureau of Regulatory Services
Department of Agriculture and
Commerce**
121 North Jefferson Street
P.O. Box 1609
Jackson, MS 39201
601-359-1111
Fax: 601-354-6502
Web site: www.mdac.state.ms.us

MISSOURI
**Consumer Protection and
Trade Offense Division**
P.O. Box 899
1530 Rax Court
Jefferson City, MO 65102
573-751-6887
573-751-3321
Toll free in MO: 800-392-8222
TDD/TTY toll free in MO:
    800-729-8668
Fax: 573-751-7948
E-mail: attgenmail@moago.org
Web site: www.ago.state.mo.us

MONTANA
**Consumer Affairs Unit
Department of Commerce**
1424 Ninth Avenue
Box 200501
Helena, MT 59620-0501
406-444-4312
Fax: 406-444-2903

NEBRASKA
Consumer Division
2115 State Capitol Building
P.O. Box 98920
Lincoln, NE 68509
402-471-2682
Toll free: 800-727-6432
Fax: 402-471-3297
Web site: www.nol.org

NEVADA
OCC/FTC

NEW HAMPSHIRE
**Consumer Protection and
Antitrust Bureau
New Hampshire Attorney
General's Office**
33 Capitol Street
Concord, NH 03301
603-271-3641
TDD toll free: 800-735-2964
Fax: 603-271-2110
Web site: www.state.nh.us/
    nhdoj/consumer/cpb.html

NEW JERSEY
**New Jersey Consumer Affairs
Division**
124 Halsey Street
P.O. Box 43027
Newark, NJ 07102
973-504-6587
973-648-6381
Fax: 973-648-3538
E-mail: browere@smtp.lps.state.
    nj.us
Web site: www.state.nj.us/lps/
    ca/home.htm

NEW MEXICO
**Consumer Protection Division
Office of the Attorney General**
P.O. Drawer 1508
407 Galisteo Street
Santa Fe, NM 87504-1508
505-827-6060
Toll free in NM: 800-678-1508
Fax: 505-827-6685
Web site: www.ago.state.nm.us

New York State Consumer Protection Board
5 Empire State Plaza, Suite 2101
Albany, NY 12223-1556
518-474-3514
518-474-8583 (capital region)
Toll free: 800-697-1220
Fax: 518-474-2474
E-mail: donna.ned@consumer.
    state.ny.us
Web site: www.consumer.state.
    ny.us

Consumer Protection Section Office of the Attorney General
P.O. Box 629
Raleigh, NC 27602
919-716-6000
Fax: 919-716-6050
Web site: www.jus.state.nc.us/
    cpframe.htm

Consumer Protection and Antitrust Division Office of the Attorney General
600 East Boulevard Avenue,
    Department 125
Bismarck, ND 58505-0040
701-328-3404
Toll free in ND: 800-472-2600
TDD: 701-328-3409
Fax: 701-328-3535
E-mail: cpat@state.nd.us
Web site: www.ag.state.nd.us/
    ndag/cpat/cpat.html

North Dakota Department of Banking and Financial Institutions
2000 Schafer Street, Suite G
Bismarck, ND 58501-1204
701-328-9933
TDD toll free in ND: 800-366-6888
Fax: 701-328-9955
E-mail: banking@state.nd.us
Web site: www.state.nd.us/bank

Ohio Attorney General's Office Consumer Protection Department
30 East Broad Street, 25th Floor
Columbus, OH 43215-3428
614-466-8831
Toll free in OH: 800-282-0515
TDD: 614-466-1393
Fax: 614-728-7583
E-mail: consumer@ag.state.oh.us
Web site: www.ag.state.oh.us

Consumer Protection Division Office of the Attorney General
440 South Houston, Suite 505
Tulsa, OK 74127-8913
918-581-2885
Web site: www.oag.state.ok.us

Financial Fraud/Consumer Protection Section Department of Justice
1162 Court Street, NE
Salem, OR 97310
503-378-4732
Hot line (Salem only):
503-378-4320
Hot line (Portland only):
503-229-5576
Toll free in OR: 877-877-9392
TDD/TTY: 503-378-5939
Fax: 503-378-5017
Web site: www.doj.state.or.us

Bureau of Consumer Protection Office of the Attorney General
Strawberry Square, 14th Floor
Harrisburg, PA 17120
717-787-9707
Toll free in PA: 800-441-2555
Fax: 717-787-1190
Web site:
www.attorneygeneral.gov

Consumer Unit Consumer Protection Unit Department of the Attorney General
150 South Main Street
Providence, RI 02903
401-274-4400
Toll free in RI: 800-852-7776
TDD: 401-453-0410
Fax: 401-222-5110

Office of the Attorney General
P.O. Box 11549
Columbia, SC 29211
803-734-3970
Fax: 803-734-3677
Web site:
www.scattorneygeneral.org

South Carolina Department of Consumer Affairs
2801 Devine Street
P.O. Box 5757
Columbia, SC 29205-5757
803-734-9452
Toll free in SC: 800-922-1594
Fax: 803-734-9365
E-mail: scdca@infoave.net
Web site: www.state.sc.us/
consumer

Office of the Attorney General
500 East Capitol
State Capitol Building
Pierre, SD 57501-5070
605-773-4400
Toll free in SD: 800-300-1986
TDD: 605-773-6585
Fax: 605-773-7163

South Dakota Division of Banking
217½ West Missouri Avenue
Pierre, SD 57501-4590
605-773-3421
Fax: 605-773-5367
Web site: www.state.sd.us/
banking

Division of Consumer Affairs
500 James Robertson Parkway,
 5th Floor
Nashville, TN 37243-0600
615-741-4737
Toll free in TN: 800-342-8385
Fax: 615-532-4994
E-mail: mwilliams2@mail.state.
 tn.us
Web site: www.state.tn.us/
 consumer

Consumer Protection Division
Office of the Attorney General
P.O. Box 12548
Austin, TX 78711-2548
512-463-2070
Fax: 512-463-8301

Consumer Protection/Houston
Regional Office
Office of the Attorney General
808 Travis, Suite 812
Houston, TX 77002
713-223-5886, ext. 118
Fax: 713-223-5821

Department of Financial
Institutions
324 South State, Suite 201
Salt Lake City, UT 84114
801-538-8830

Consumer Assistance Program
for Consumer Complaints and
Questions
104 Morrill Hall
UVM
Burlington, VT 05405
802-656-3183
Toll free in VT: 800-649-2424

Office of Consumer Affairs
Department of Agriculture
and Consumer Services
Washington Building, Suite 100
P.O. Box 1163
Richmond, VA 23219
804-786-2042
Toll free in VA: 800-552-9963
TDD: 800-828-1120
Fax: 804-371-7479
Web site: www.vdacs.state.va.us

Consumer Resource Center
Office of the Attorney General
103 East Holly Street, Suite 308
Bellingham, WA 98225-4728
360-738-6185

Consumer Resource Center
Office of the Attorney General
500 North Morain Street,
 Suite 1250
Kennewick, WA 99336-2607
509-734-2967

Consumer Resource Center
Office of the Attorney General
905 Plum Street, Building 3
P.O. Box 40118
Olympia, WA 98504-0118
360-753-6210

Consumer Resource Center
Office of the Attorney General
900 Fourth Avenue, Suite 2000
Seattle, WA 98164-1012
206-464-6684
Toll free in WA: 800-551-4636
   (Consumer Resource Centers)
TDD toll free in WA: 800-276-9883
Fax: 206-464-6451
Web site: www.wa.gov/ago

Consumer Resource Center
Office of the Attorney General
1116 West Riverside Avenue
Spokane, WA 99201-1194
509-456-3123

Consumer Resource Center
Office of the Attorney General
Consumer Protection Division
1019 Pacific Avenue, 3rd Floor
Tacoma, WA 98402-4411
253-593-2904
Toll free: 800-551-4636
Toll free in WA only: 800-276-9883
Fax: 253-593-2449
E-mail: cynthial@atg.wa.gov
Web site: www.wa.gov/ago

Consumer Resource Center
Office of the Attorney General
1220 Main Street, Suite 510
Vancouver, WA 98660
360-759-2150

Consumer Protection Division
Office of the Attorney General
812 Quarrier Street, 6th Floor
P.O. Box 1789
Charleston, WV 25326-1789
304-558-8986
Toll free in WV: 800-368-8808
Fax: 304-558-0184
E-mail: consumer@wvnet.edu
Web site: www.state.wv.us/
   wvag/index0816.html

Division of Trade and
Consumer Protection
Department of Agriculture
Trade and Consumer
Protection
3610 Oakwood Hills Parkway
Eau Claire, WI 54701-7754
715-839-3848
Toll free in WI: 800-422-7128
Fax: 715-839-1645

Wisconsin Department of
AgricultureTrade and
Consumer Protection
200 North Jefferson Street,
   Suite 146-A
Green Bay, WI 54301
920-448-5111
920-448-5114
Toll free in WI: 800-422-7128
Fax: 920-448-5118
Web site:
   www.badger.state.wi.us/
   agencies/datcp

**Division of Trade and
Consumer Protection
Department of Agriculture**
2811 Agriculture Drive
P.O. Box 8911
Madison, WI 53708
608-224-4953
Toll free in WI: 800-422-7128
TTD/TTY: 608-224-5058
Fax: 608-224-4939
E-mail: datephotline@wheel.
datep.state.wi.us
Web site: www.datcp.state.wi.us

**Office of the Attorney General
Consumer Protection Unit**
123 State Capitol Building
Cheyenne, WY 82002
307-777-7874
Toll free in WY only: 800-438-5799
Fax: 307-777-7956
E-mail: cpetri@state.wy.us
Web site: www.state.wy.us/
ag/consumer.htm

Appendix C:
Transportation Agencies

Alabama Department of Transportation
1409 Coliseum Boulevard
P.O. Box 303050
Montgomery, AL 36130-3050
334-242-6358
Web site: www.dot.state.al.us

ALASKA

Alaska Department of Transportation and Public Facilities
3132 Channel Drive
Juneau, AK 99801-7898
907-465-3900
Web site: www.dot.state.ak.us/
external/tmphome.html

ARIZONA

Arizona Department of Transportation
206 South 17th Avenue
Phoenix, AZ 85007
602-712-7011
Web site: www.dot.state.az.us

ARKANSAS

Arkansas State Highway and Transportation Department
Mailing Address:
P.O. Box 2261
Little Rock, AR 72203

Street Address:
10324 Interstate 30
Little Rock, AR 72209
501-569-2000
Web site: www.ahtd.state.ar.us

CALIFORNIA

California Department of Transportation
Mailing Address:
P.O. Box 942873
Sacramento, CA 94273-0001

Street Address:
1120 N Street
Sacramento, CA
916-654-5266
Web site: www.dot.ca.gov

COLORADO

Colorado Department of Transportation
Office of Public Information
4201 East Arkansas Avenue
Denver, CO 80222
303-757-9011
Web site: www.dot.state.co.us

Connecticut Department of Transportation
2800 Berlin Turnpike
Newington, CT 06131-7546
860-594-2000
Web site: www.dot.state.ct.us

Delaware Department of Transportation
P.O. Box 778
Dover, DE 19903
302-760-2080
800-652-5600
Web site: www.state.de.us/
deldot/index.html

District Division of Transportation
2000 14th Street, NW, 6th Floor
Washington, DC 20009
202-673-6813
Fax: 202-671-0642
Web site: www.ddot.dc.gov

Florida Department of Transportation
605 Suwannee Street
Tallahassee, FL 32399-0450
850-414-4100
Web site: www.dot.state.fl.us

Georgia Department of Transportation
2 Capitol Square, Room 106
Atlanta, GA 30334
404-656-5211
Web site: www.dot.state.ga.us

State of Hawaii Department of Transportation
Aliiaimoku Building
869 Punchbowl Street
Honolulu, HI 96813
808-587-2150
Web site: www.hawaii.gov/dot

Idaho Transportation Department
3311 West State Street
Boise, ID 83707-1129
208-334-8000
Web site: www2.state.id.us/itd/
index.htm

Illinois Department of Transportation
2300 South Dirksen Parkway
Springfield, IL 62764
217-782-7820
Web site: www.dot.state.il.us

Indiana Department of Transportation
100 North Senate Avenue,
Room IGCN 755
Indianapolis, IN 46204
317-232-5533
Web site: www.state.in.us/dot

Iowa Department of Transportation
800 Lincoln Way
Ames, IA 50010
515-239-1101
Fax: 515-239-1639
Web site: www.dot.state.ia.us

Kansas Department of Transportation
915 Harrison, Room 754
Docking State Office Building
Topeka, KS 66612-1568
785-296-3585
Web site: www.ink.org/
  public/kdot

Kentucky Transportation Cabinet
501 High Street
Frankfort, KY 40601
502-564-4890
Web site: www.kytc.state.ky.us

Louisiana Department of Transportation and Development
Mailing Address:
P.O. Box 94245
Baton Rouge, LA 70804-9245

Street Address:
1201 Capitol Access Road
Baton Rouge, LA 70802-4438
225-379-1100
Web site: www.dotd.state.la.us

Maine Department of Transportation
16 State House Station
Augusta, ME 04333
207-287-2551
Web site: www.state.me.us/mdot

Maryland Department of Transportation
P.O. Box 8755
BWI Airport, MD 21240
888-713-1414
Fax: 410-865-1334
Web site: www.mdot.state.
  md.us/index.html

Massachusetts Highway Department
10 Park Plaza
Boston, MA 02116
617-973-7541
Web site: www.state.ma.us/mhd

Michigan Department of Transportation
State Transportation Building
425 West Ottawa Street
P.O. Box 30050
Lansing, MI 48909
517-373-2090
Web site: www.mdot.state.mi.us

Minnesota Department of Transportation
Transportation Building
395 John Ireland Boulevard
St. Paul, MN 55155 _
651-296-3000
Web site: www.dot.state.mn.us

Mississippi Department of Transportation
Mailing Address:
P.O. Box 1850
Jackson, MS 39215-1850

Street Address:
401 North West Street
Jackson, MS 39201
601-359-7001
Fax: 601-359-7050
Web site: www.mdot.state.ms.us

Missouri Department of Transportation
105 West Capitol Avenue
P.O. Box 270
Jefferson City, MO 65102
573-751-2551
Web site: www.modot.state.mo.us

Montana Department of Transportation
P.O. Box 201001
2701 Prospect Avenue
Helena, MT 59620-1001
406-444-6200
Web site: www.mdt.state.mt.us

Nebraska Department of Roads
P.O. Box 94759
Lincoln, NE 68509-4759
402-471-4567
Web site: www.dor.state.ne.us

Nevada Department of Transportation
1263 South Stewart Street
Carson City, NV 89712
775-888-7000
Fax: 775-888-7115
Web site: www.nevadadot.com

New Hampshire Department of Transportation
John O. Morton Building
1 Hazen Drive
Concord, NH 03302-0483
603-271-3734
Web site: www.state.nh.us/dot/
index.html

New Jersey Department of Transportation
1035 Parkway Avenue
P.O. Box 600
Trenton, NJ 08625
609-530-2000
Web site: www.state.nj.us/
transportation

New Mexico State Highway and Transportation Department
6401 South Tucson Boulevard
Tucson, NM 85706
520-746-4500
Web site: www.nmshtd.state.
nm.us/start/default.asp

New York State Department of Transportation
1220 Washington Avenue
Harriman Campus Building 5,
    Room 506
Albany, NY 12232
518-457-4422
Web site: www.dot.state.ny.us

North Carolina Department of Transportation
Mailing Address:
1501 Mail Service Center
Raleigh, NC 27699-1501

Street Address:
1 South Wilmington Street
Raleigh, NC 27601
919-733-2520
Web site: www.dot.state.nc.us

North Dakota Department of Transportation
608 East Boulevard Avenue
Bismarck, ND 58505-0700
701-328-2500
Web site: www.state.nd.us/dot

Ohio Department of Transportation
1980 West Broad Street
Columbus, OH 43223
614-466-7170
Fax: 614-644-8662
Web site: www.dot.state.oh.us

Oklahoma Department of Transportation
200 NE 21st Street
Oklahoma City, OK 73105
405-521-2528
Web site: www.okladot.state.ok.us

Oregon Department of Transportation
355 Capitol Street NE
Salem, OR 97301-3871
888-ASK-ODOT (888-245-6368)
Web site: www.odot.state.or.us

Pennsylvania Department of Transportation
Keystone Building
400 North Street
Harrisburg, PA 17120
717-787-2838
Web site: www.dot.state.pa.us

Rhode Island Department of Transportation
Two Capitol Hill
Providence, RI 02903-1124
401-222-1362
Web site: www.dot.state.ri.us

South Carolina Department of Transportation
955 Park Street
P.O. Box 191
Columbia, SC 29292-0191
803-737-2314
Web site: www.dot.state.sc.us

South Dakota Department of Transportation
700 East Broadway Avenue
Becker-Hansen Building
Pierre, SD 57501
605-773-3265
Web site: www.state.sd.us/dot

Tennessee Department of Transportation
505 Deaderick Street, Suite 700
James K. Polk Building
Nashville, TN 37243
615-741-2848
Web site: www.tdot.state.tn.us

Texas Department of Transportation
125 East 11th Street
Austin, TX 78701-2483
512-416-2000
Web site: www.dot.state.tx.us

Utah Department of Transportation
4501 South 2700 West
Salt Lake City, UT 84119-5998
801-965-4000
Fax: 801-965-4391
Web site: www.sr.ex.state.ut.us

Vermont Agency of Transportation
1 National Life Drive, Drawer 33
Montpelier, VT 05633
802-828-2657
Fax: 802-828-3522
Web site: www.aot.state.vt.us

Virginia Department of Transportation
1401 East Broad Street
Richmond, VA 23219
804-786-2716
Web site: www.vdot.state.va.us

Washington State Department of Transportation
310 Maple Park Avenue, SE
Olympia, WA 98501-2361
360-705-7000
Web site: www.wsdot.wa.gov

West Virginia Department of Transportation
1900 Kanawha Boulevard,
   Building 5
Charleston, WV 25305
304-558-2530
Fax: 304-558-1004
Web site: www.wvdot.com

Wisconsin Department of Transportation
Office of Public Affairs
P.O. Box 70910
Madison, WI 53707-7910
608-266-3581
Web site: www.dot.state.wi.us

Wyoming Department of Transportation
5300 Bishop Boulevard
Cheyenne, WY 82009-3340
307-777-4375
Web site: www.wydotweb.
   state.wy.us

Appendix D:
Credit Reporting Agencies

EQUIFAX

www.equifax.com

Consumers' address for credit reports:
Equifax Credit Information Services, Inc.
P.O. Box 740241
Atlanta, GA 30374
800-356-4715

TRANSUNION, LLC

www.transunion.com

Consumers' address for credit reports:
TransUnion, LLC
P.O. Box 2000
Chester, PA 19022
800-888-4213

EXPERIAN

www.experian.com

Consumers' address for credit reports:
Experian
P.O. Box 2002
Allen, TX 75013
888-397-3742

Fees for someone to request his own credit report are controlled in part by the Fair Credit Reporting Act, which increased the fee to $8.50 plus any applicable taxes. Residents of some states have lesser or greater fees.

INDEX

A

account numbers, 93, 170

account reconciliation, 171

addressee, 38

addresses, 93

admissions, 72, 77

advertising, 220

agencies:
 credit reporting, 329
 federal, 259–60
 state banking, 296–304
 state consumer
  protection, 261–74
 state education, 305–12
 state transportation, 323–8

airlines:
 additional cost of later
  flights, 226–8
 canceled or delayed
  flights, 227
 overbooked flights, 229–31

Airline Service
 Complaints, 259

Alabama:
 Center for Commerce,
  Superintendent of
  Banks, 296
 Consumer Affairs
  Division, 261, 313
 Education Department,
  305
 Insurance Department,
  289

small claims courts in,
 247
Transportation
 Department, 323

Alaska:
 Commerce Department,
  296
 Community and Economic
  Development
  Department, 289
 Consumer Protection
  Unit, 261, 313
 Education and Early
  Development
  Department, 305
 Insurance Division, 289
 small claims courts in,
  247
 Transportation and Public
  Facilities Department,
  323

Americans with
 Disabilities Act (ADA),
 209

appropriate legal action,
 30, 66, 138, 168

Arizona:
 Banking Department, 296
 Consumer Protection
  Division, 261
 Education Department,
  305
 Insurance Department,
  275, 289
 small claims courts in,
  247
 Transportation
  Department, 323

Arkansas:
 Bank Department, 296

Consumer Protection
 Division, 261, 313
Education Department,
 305
Highway and
 Transportation
 Department, 323
Insurance Department,
 289
small claims courts in,
 248

assurances, 180

attorneys, see lawyers

audience, knowing your,
 11

automobile dealers:
 settlement agreement on
  repairing defective car,
  242–3
 see also cars

B

"bad faith," 25

balances, unpaid, 167

banking agencies, state,
 296–304

bankruptcy, 174

banks, 154–8
 checking account
  problems and, 154–6
 errors on statements
  from, 157–8

bargaining, 165

"baseless," 25, 234

bills, credit card:
 botched, 170–1
 corrections of, 167–69

"breach," 25
 of warranty, 54

building, faulty, 83–5
bundling, 122
businesses, aid from, 80
buzzwords, 23–7, 53, 85, 86, 111, 183, 188, 203

C

cable service
   complaints, with FCC, 259–60
California:
   Attorney General's Office, 262
   Automotive Repair Bureau, 262
   Consumer Affairs Department, 261
   Education Department, 305
   Financial Institutions Department, 296
   Insurance Department, 289
   Managed Healthcare Department, 276
   Public Inquiry Unit, 314
   small claims courts in, 248
   Transportation Department, 323
canceled checks, 156
canceled flights, 227
car dealers, settlement agreement on repairing defective transmissions, 242–3
care, standard of, 24, 26

car manufacturers, defective cars and, 51–3
cars:
   damaged in parking lot, 59–61
   defective, 51–3
   safety complaints, with NHTSA, 260
   used, 57–8
case, presentation of, 7
caterers, 88–90
cc ("carbon copy to"), 7, 16, 41 50, 53, 68, 80, 162, 166, 243
cease and desist, 182–8
certified mail, return receipt requested, 14, 40, 51, 81, 113, 125, 127, 132, 151, 157, 161, 184, 191, 196, 197, 200, 236, 237
checking account problems, banks and, 154–6
checks, canceled, 156
children, school problems of, 197–202
city agencies, 61
Civil Rights Division of the Department of Justice, 259
claims:
   legal basis for, 224
   procedures for, 162
   unjustified, 184–6

collection agencies:
   attempts to collect money not owed, 187–8
   unjustified claims by, 184–6
collections, 182–3, 189–92
   of money owed for work, 189–90
Colorado:
   Consumer Protection Division, 262
   Education Department, 305
   Insurance Division, 276, 289
   small claims courts in, 248–9
   State Bank Commissioner, 296
   Transportation Department, 323
compensatory damages, 203
condescension, 29
conditions, dangerous or damaging, 76
Connecticut:
   Antitrust/Consumer Protection, 262, 314
   Banking Department, 297
   Consumer Protection Department, 262, 314
   Education Department, 306
   Insurance Department, 276, 290
   small claims courts in, 249
   Transportation Department, 324

consequences,
consequential
damages, 17, 130
constituents, 139, 146
construction
management, 84
consumer complaints,
against credit card
companies, 313–22
Consumer Information
Center, 259
Consumer Product
Safety Commission, 251
consumer protection,
1–2
agencies, 41, 168, 259,
261–74
threats and, 32
contingent fees, 135,
185, 189
contractors:
bonds of, 66
faulty additions built by,
83–5
general, 84
HVAC, 67–8
installation of hazardous
garage doors by, 86–7
responding to threatened
lawsuits, 234–5
subcontractors, 84
contracts:
canceled, 91–2
insurance claims and,
99–100, 104
reading relevant
provisions in, 162
state laws on, 92

copies:
of documents, 138, 179,
202; see also
Enclosures
of letters, see cc ("carbon
copy to")
unnecessary, 58, 144,
199
corrections, 77
correct person, 93, 145,
154, 167, 212
costs:
additional, 226–8
legal, 166
replacement and repair,
70
County Council member,
public works and,
139–41
county sanitation
department, poor
garbage removal
service and, 145–6
county school board,
negligent school bus
drivers and, 203–4
courts:
small claims, 27, 73, 82,
247–57
traffic, 150–3
co-workers, sexual
harassment and,
214–6
credit card companies:
bill corrections refused
by, 167–9
botched bills from,
170–1

consumer complaints
against, 313–22
merchants and, 168
unannounced changes
in interest rates by,
176–7
credit cards:
department store, 180–1
disputed charges on, 222
hotels and, 222
and unsatisfactory
purchases, 43, 167–9
creditors, payment
delays and, 174–5
credit reporting
companies, 167, 237,
329
harmful information filed
by, 238–40
credit reports, obtaining,
237
customer relations
managers, 154, 227
Customs, U.S., 260

D

damages, 88, 92, 94
compensatory, 203
consequential, 17
documentation of, 61
punitive, 203
damaging conditions,
76
dangerous conditions,
76
dealers, defective
merchandise and,
45–6, 242–3

debtors, payment
  arrangements for, 174
defects, defective, 28,
  32, 63
  installations, 86–7,
    242–4
  merchandise, 38–9,
    45–6, 51–3, 87,
    244–6
  repairs, 76–7
  work, 63, 65, 81–2
defense, letters in your,
  236–8
Delaware:
  Bank Commissioner,
    Office of State, 297, 314
  Consumer Protection
    Unit, 262
  Education Department,
    306
  Fraud and Consumer
    Protection Division, 262
  Health Facilities,
    Licensing, and
    Certification (health
    claims review), 277
  Insurance Department,
    290
  small claims courts in,
    249
  Transportation
    Department, 324
delay, consequences of,
  130
delayed flights, 227
demands, 17, 155
denial, wrongful, 23, 24
department store credit
  cards, 180–1

discrimination
  complaints, with Civil
    Rights Division of
    Justice Department,
    259
District of Columbia:
  Banking and Financial
    Institutions Office, 297,
    314
  Corporation Counsel's
    Office, 262
  Health Department,
    Grievance and Appeals,
    277
  Insurance and Securities
    Regulation Department,
    290
  Public Schools, 306
  small claims courts in,
    249
  Transportation Division,
    324
documents,
  documentation, 18,
  19, 114, 121, 162,
  164, 173
  copies of, 138, 178, 201;
    see also Enclosures
  of damages, 61
  of facts, 18
  of opponent's refusal,
    19
  see also paper trail
dry cleaners, 73–5

E

economics, 66
education agencies,
  state, 305–12

elected representatives,
  149
e-mail, letters vs., 13
emotions, and legal
  action, 6, 53
employee handbooks, on
  sexual harassment, 211
employers:
  and co-workers,
    211–8
  and requests for
    promotion, 217–8
  sexual harassment and,
    211–3
enclosures, 39, 70, 202
Equifax, 329
estimates, 61
evidence, 18, 73
exculpatory clauses, 60
Experian, 329
expert opinion, 20, 22,
  58, 82, 85, 110, 115,
  194, 196

F

factors, 173
facts, 98, 146
  of case, 18
  documentation of, 18
  of legal cases, 6
faulty work, 62–4
fax machines, 95
federal agencies, 54,
  179, 188, 210, 212,
  227, 259–60
Federal Bureau of
  Investigation (FBI), 259

Federal Communications
Commission (FCC), 259
Federal Express, 108
federal laws:
  on debt collection, 185,
  188
  on sexual harassment,
  211
Federal Trade
Commission (FTC),
260, 313
fees, contingent, 135
fiscal intermediaries,
133
flights:
  canceled or delayed,
  227
  later, 226-8
  overbooked, 229-31
Florida:
  Agriculture and Consumer
  Services Department,
  263, 314
  Banking and Finance,
  297
  Economic Crimes
  Division, 263
  Education Department,
  306
  Insurance Department,
  290
  Multi-State Litigation,
  263
  small claims courts in,
  249
  Statewide Provider and
  Subscriber Assistance
  Program (health claims
  review), 277

Transportation
Department, 324
follow-up letters, 8, 40,
127-8, 163-6, 178-9,
200-2
Food and Drug
Administration (FDA),
260
food poisoning, 137-8
form, for guilty pleas, 151
format, for letters, 12-6
fraud, 43
friends, money owed by,
191-2
furniture, trucking
companies and damage
to, 69-70

G

garbage removal service,
poor, 145-6
garden service, careless
performance by, 71-2
general contractors, 84
Georgia:
  Banking and Finance
  Department, 297
  Consumer Affairs
  Department, 263, 314
  Education Department,
  306
  Health Planning Agency,
  278
  Insurance Department,
  290
  small claims courts in,
  250

Transportation
Department, 324
goals, of legal cases, 2,
6
goods and services,
38-94
goodwill, 39
government agencies,
139-53
government official,
threatened action by,
232-3
grammar, 13
"gross negligence,"
"grossly negligent," 24,
26, 60, 203
"groundless," 25, 234
guardians, legal, 118
guilty, plea of, 151

H

harassment, 183, 188
  sexual, see sexual
  harassment
  telephone calls as,
  182-3
harm, 195
Hawaii:
  Consumer Protection
  Offices, 263, 314
  Education Department,
  306
  Financial Institutions,
  Commissioner of, 297
  Insurance Division, 278,
  290
  small claims courts in,
  250

Transportation
Department, 324
"hazardous," 25, 27, 86
installations, 86-7
health care, 95-133
health care providers,
see HMOs
health claims decisions,
state independent
review panels for,
275-87
health problems,
referring to, 195, 206
hearings, before state
agencies, 165
history of events,
written, 94, 143, 149
HMOs, 96-133
deviation from approved
procedures of, 124
extensive medical care
and, 101-4
independent review
panels for health claims,
275-87
medical care for
incompetent son by,
118-9
medical care needed
outside network of,
108-12
medical devices
demanded from,
113-5
medical reimbursements
and, 98-100
overpayment claims and,
120-1
physicians vs., 97

referral to specialist by,
105-7
refusal to pay for service,
122-4
request for additional
physical therapy,
131-3
request for change of
primary care physician,
110-1
request for tests prior to
use of medication,
125-30
"standard of care" and,
28, 30
holders in due course,
173
hotels:
bad service in, 221-2
reservations not honored
by, 223-5
humor, 137
HVAC contractors, 67-8

I

Idaho:
Consumer Protection
Unit, 263, 315
Education Department,
306
Finance Department, 298
Insurance Department,
290
small claims courts in,
250
Transportation
Department, 324
Illinois:
Attorney General's Office,
264

Banks and Real Estate
Office, 298
Board of Education, 307
Consumer Fraud Bureau,
264
Consumer Protection
Division of the Attorney
General's Office, 264
Governor's Office of
Citizens' Assistance, 264
Insurance Department,
278, 290
small claims courts in,
250
Transportation
Department, 324
"improperly trained,"
25
incompetence, mental,
118-9
Indiana:
Consumer Protection
Division, 264, 315
Education Department,
307
Financial Institutions
Department, 298
Insurance Department,
291
Insurance Department,
Health Issues Division,
279
small claims courts in,
250
Transportation
Department, 324
indifference, reckless,
24
individuals, 38
inspection, 70

installations, defective,
86-7, 234-5
insults, 29
insurance claims:
  contracts and, 99, 104
  health, and independent
    review panels, 275-87
  procedures for, 162
insurance commissions,
  state, 289-95
insurance companies:
  personal injury claims
    and, 136
  physicians vs., 97
  theft coverage by,
    161-6
insurance salesman,
  policy copy not
  provided by, 159-60
interest rates,
  unannounced changes
  by credit cards in,
  176-9
Internal Revenue
  Service, erroneous tax
  refund, 142-4
interstate commerce,
  220
Iowa:
  Banking Division, 298
  Consumer Protection
    Division, 264, 315
  Education Department,
    307
  Insurance Division, 279,
    291
  small claims courts in,
    250

Transportation
  Department, 324

J

jackets, ruined, 73-5
job performance, 217
joint tax returns,
  signatures for, 144
Justice Department,
  U.S., Civil Rights
  Division of, 259

K

Kansas:
  Bank Commissioner, 298
  Consumer Protection
    Division, 264, 315
  District Attorney's Office,
    265
  Education Department,
    307
  Insurance Department,
    279, 291
  small claims courts in,
    250-1
  Transportation
    Department, 325
Kentucky:
  Consumer Protection
    Division, 265, 315
  Education Department,
    307
  Financial Institutions
    Department, 299
  Insurance Department,
    280, 291
  small claims courts in,
    251
  Transportation Cabinet,
    325

L

Labor Department, U.S.,
  259
ladder of authority, 146
landlords, 207-9
  security deposits not
    returned by, 207-8
  settlement agreement on
    repairs to apartment by,
    239-41
laws, see federal laws;
  state laws
lawsuits, 2-5, 92
  threatened, 28-31, 46,
    58, 61, 68, 72, 82, 90,
    185, 190, 208, 244-6
lawyers, 73, 135, 166,
  240
  copies of correspondence
    to, 166
  reference to, 72
  reimbursement for, 166
  techniques used by, 2-3
  thinking like, 5-8
  threatening with, 46, 90
  traffic court and, 150
  unjustified claims by,
    184-6
leases, 240
  provisions of, 208
legal action, 196, 245
  appropriate, 33, 66, 138,
    168
  see also lawsuits
legal arguments, 160
legal assistance, threat
  of, 46, 90
legal basis for claim, 224

legal consequences, 183
legal costs, 166
legal guardians, 118
legal violations, 87
"lemon," 24, 53
letters:
  appropriate tone in, 9–10,
    29, 132, 192, 194
  concision in, 9
  effective, 2–3, 9–36
  e-mail vs., 13
  faxing of, 95
  follow-up, 40
  format for, 11–15
  hand-delivery of, 150, 217
  ineffective, 21, 33
  knowing audience of, 11
  and knowing your rights,
    11
  making your case in,
    16–28
  read by others, 140
  samples, 37–246
  settlement, 36
  simplicity in, 10–11
liability, 134–8
licenses, 68
local dealers:
  defective cars and, 51–3
  lack of response by,
    47–50
  national dealers and,
    47–50
local offices, national
  offices vs., 164, 224
logic, 14
Louisiana:
  Consumer Protection
    Section, 265, 315

Education Department,
  307
Financial Institutions
  Office, 299
Insurance Department,
  280, 291
small claims courts in,
  251
Transportation and
  Development
  Department, 325

M

mail fraud complaints,
  260
mail order, 42–4
Maine:
  Banking, Superintendent
    of, 299
  Consumer Credit
    Regulation Office, 265,
    316
  Consumer Mediation
    Service, Attorney
    General's, 265
  Education Department,
    307
  Insurance Bureau, 280,
    291
  Public Protection Division,
    265
  small claims courts in,
    251
  Transportation
    Department, 325
"malicious," 25, 234
"malpractice," 24, 27,
  111
management,
  construction, 84

manufacturers:
  car, 51–3
  television, 54–6
  warranties, 46
Maryland:
  Business Licensing and
    Consumer Service, 267
  Consumer Protection
    Division, 266, 316
  Education Department,
    307
  Financial Regulation
    Division, 299
  Insurance Administration,
    291
  Insurance Commission,
    280
  small claims courts in,
    251
  Transportation
    Department, 325
masons, defective work
  by, 81–2
Massachusetts:
  Banks, Division of, 299
  Consumer Affairs and
    Business Regulation
    Office, 266
  Consumer Protection and
    Antitrust Division, 266,
    316
  Education Department,
    308
  Highway Department,
    325
  Insurance Division,
    291
  Public Health
    Department, Office of
    Patient Protection,
    281

small claims courts in, 251

medical care:
critical need for, 111
extensive, HMOs and, 101–4
for incompetent son, 118–9
outside HMO network, 108–12
standard of, 28, 30

medical devices, 113–5

medical malpractice, 111

medical questions, private consultations and, 103

medical reimbursements, HMOs and, 98–100

medical testing, 121
prior to use of medication, 125–30

medication:
monitoring of, 117
testing prior to, 125–30

mental incompetence, 118–9

merchandise, defective, 38–41, 45–6, 51–3, 85, 244–6

merchants:
credit card companies and, 168
time payments not credited by, 172–3

Michigan:
Automotive Regulation Bureau, 266
Consumer Protection Division, 266, 316
Education Department, 308
Financial and Insurance Services Office, 281
Financial Institutions Bureau, 299
Insurance Bureau, 292
small claims courts in, 251
Transportation Department, 325

Minnesota:
Children, Families, and Learning Department, 308
Commerce Department, 292, 300
Consumer Services Division, 266, 316
Managed Health Care Program Ombudsman, 281
small claims courts in, 251–2
Transportation Department, 325

misleading material, 43

misrepresentation, 220

Mississippi:
Banking and Consumer Finance Department, 300
Bureau of Regulatory Services, 267, 317
Consumer Protection Division, 267, 316

Education Department, 308
Insurance Department, 292
small claims courts in, 252
Transportation Department, 326

Missouri:
Consumer Protection and Trade Offense Division, 267, 317
Elementary and Secondary Education Department, 308
Finance Department, 300
Insurance Department, 282, 292
small claims courts in, 252
Transportation Department, 326

money:
in business situations, 3–4
owed by friends and relatives, 191–2
owed for work, 189–90

Montana:
Banking and Financial Institutions Division, 300
Consumer Affairs Unit, 267, 317
Insurance Department, 292
Public Health and Human Services Department, 282
Public Instruction Office, 308

small claims courts in, 252

Transportation Department, 326

N

national dealers, local dealers and, 47–50

National Highway Traffic Safety Administration, 260

national offices, local offices vs., 164, 224

Nebraska:
 Banking and Finance Department, 300
 Consumer Division, 317
 Education Department, 308
 Insurance Department, 282, 292
 Justice Department, 267
 Roads Department, 326
 small claims courts in, 252

"negligence," "negligent," 24, 26, 135
 gross, 24, 26, 60, 203

neighbors, 193–6
 offensive, 195–6
 property line disputes with, 193–4

Nevada:
 Bureau of Consumer Protection, 267
 Business and Industry Department, Financial Institutions Division, 300

Consumer Affairs Division, 267–8

Education Department, 309

Insurance Division, 292

small claims courts in, 252

Transportation Department, 326

New Hampshire:
 Banking Department, 301
 Consumer Protection and Antitrust Bureau, 268, 317
 Education Department, 309
 Insurance Department, 283, 292
 small claims courts in, 252
 Transportation Department, 326

New Jersey:
 Banking and Insurance Department, 301
 Consumer Affairs Division, 268, 317
 Division of Law, 268
 Education Department, 309
 Health and Senior Services, Commissioner of, 283
 Insurance Department, 292
 small claims courts in, 253
 Transportation Department, 326

New Mexico:
 Consumer Protection Division, 268, 317
 Education Department, 309
 Financial Institutions Division, 301
 Highway and Transportation Department, 326
 Insurance Department, 293
 small claims courts in, 253

New York:
 Banking Department, 301
 Consumer Frauds and Protection Bureau, 268–9
 Consumer Protection Board, 269, 318
 Education Department, 309
 Insurance Department, 283, 293
 small claims courts in, 253
 Transportation Department, 327

noise problems, 195–6

North Carolina:
 Banks, Commissioner of, 301
 Consumer Protection Section, 269, 318
 Insurance Department, 293
 Public Instruction Department, 309
 small claims courts in, 253–4
 Transportation Department, 327

North Dakota:
Attorney General's Office, 269
Banking and Financial Institutions Department, 301, 318
Consumer Protection and Antitrust Division, 269, 318
Insurance Department, 293
Public Instruction Department, 310
small claims courts in, 254
Transportation Department, 327

O

office buildings, wheelchair inaccessibility of, 209–10
Office of the Comptroller of Currency (OCC), 313, 314, 315, 317
Ohio:
Attorney General's Office, 269
Commerce Department, 302
Consumer Protection Department, 318
Consumers' Counsel, 270
Education Department, 310
Insurance Department, 284, 293
small claims courts in, 254

Transportation Department, 327
Oklahoma:
Attorney General, 270
Banking Department, 302
Consumer Credit Department, 270
Consumer Protection Division, 270, 318
Education Department, 310
Health Department, 284
Insurance Department, 293
small claims courts in, 254
Transportation Department, 327
Oregon:
Consumer and Business Services Department, 302
Education Department, 310
Financial Fraud/ Consumer Protection Section, 270, 319
Insurance Division, 293
small claims courts in, 254
Transportation Department, 327
overpayment claims, HMOs and, 120–1

P

paper trail, 8
creation of, 105
paperwork, 18, 171

parking lots, cars damaged in, 59–61
payments:
delays in, 174–5
HMO's refusal of, 122–4
promise of, 189–90
time, 172–3
Pennsylvania:
Banking Department, 302
Consumer Advocate's Office, 270
Consumer Protection Bureau, 270, 319
Education Department, 310
Health Department, 284
Insurance Department, 293
small claims courts in, 254
Transportation Department, 327
performance:
careless, 71–2
substantial, 25
personal injury, 134–6
phone calls, unreturned, 63
physical therapy, HMO request for, 131–3
physicians, primary care:
patients' relationships with, 95
on patient vs. health care provider, 115
request for change of, 116–7
telephone calls unreturned by, 95–7

vs. HMOs and insurance companies, 97
see also medical care
plumbers:
defective repairs by, 76–7
faulty work by, 62–4
police officers, integrity of, 150
policy numbers, 161
Postal Crime Hotline, 260
primary care physicians, see physicians, primary care
principal, public school, child's problems and, 197–202
private consultations, medical questions and, 103
procedures, for insurance claims, 162
products, defective, 38–41, 45–6, 51–3, 87, 244–6
property line disputes, 193–4
public agencies, 80, 100, 139–153, 232–3
correct person at, 145
public employees, 198
public officials, 41, 139
public rights, 198
public schools, child's problems at, 197–202

public works, 139–41
punitive damages, 203

Q

quid pro quo sexual harassment, 211
quotes, 72, 77

R

radar detectors, 150
reasonable:
alternatives, 206
persons, 122, 196
reliance, 180
receipts, 75, 138
"reckless indifference," 24
recklessness, 60
recommendations, 64
record keeping, 27, 62
references, 217
referrals, by HMOs to specialists, 105–7
refunds, limitations on, 43
regulatory agencies, 54
reimbursements, 89
medical, HMOs and, 98–100
relatives, money owed by, 191–2
reliance, reasonable, 180
remedies, 71
repairs, 239–41, 242–3, 244–6
defective, 76–7

replacement and repair costs, 70
representation of larger group, 149
reputation, 39, 224
responses:
lack of, 47–50
request for specific, 192
responsibility, 72
restaurants, bad food served by, 137–8
retailers, defective items and, 38–41
revenge, in legal cases, 2
Rhode Island:
Banking, Associate Director and Superintendent of, 302
Consumer Protection Unit, 271, 319
Elementary and Secondary Education Department, 310
Health Department, 285
Insurance Division, 294
small claims courts in, 254
Transportation Department, 327
rights:
to education, 198
knowing your, 11
roofers, settlement agreement on installation of defective roofs, 244–6

S

sales, cancellation of, 160

salesmen, insurance, 159–60

sanitation department, county, poor garbage removal service, 145–6

school, 197–206
child teased in, 197–202
and negligent bus drivers, 203–4
special accommodation for child in, 205–6

second opinions, 121

security deposit, 207–8

services, goods and, 38–94

settlement agreement letters, 35, 136, 239–46

sexual harassment:
co-workers and, 214–6
employers and, 211–3
quid pro quo, 211
sexually charged workplace and, 211

signatures, for joint tax returns, 144

small claims courts, 27, 73, 82, 247–58

social security numbers, 142

South Carolina:
Attorney General's Office, 271, 319
Consumer Affairs Department, 271, 319
Education Department, 310
Executive Policy and Program Office, 271
Financial Institutions Board, 302
Insurance Department, 285, 294
small claims courts in, 254–5
Transportation Department, 327

South Dakota:
Attorney General's Office, 271, 319
Banking Division, 302, 319
Education and Cultural Affairs Department, 311
Insurance Division, 294
small claims courts in, 255
Transportation Department, 328

special accommodation, in schools, 205–6

specialists, HMO referrals to, 105–7

specific harm, 94

spelling, 13

spokespeople, group, 127

"standard of care," 24, 26

state agencies, 33–5, 54, 61, 68, 129, 149, 179, 188, 210, 212, 227, 237
attorney generals' offices, 243
banking, 158, 296–304
for consumer complaints, 313–22
consumer protection, 168, 180, 261–74
credit card offices, 179
education, 305–12
health claims review boards, 275–8
health offices, 99, 105
hearings before, 166
insurance commissions, 160, 164, 166, 289–95
review boards, 96, 111
tax authorities, 144
transportation, 323–8

state laws, 160
on contracts, 92
on debt collection, 185, 188
on sexual harassment, 211

stoplight installation, request to state traffic department for, 147–9

store, slip and fall in, 134–6

subcontractors, 84

"substantial performance," 25

suit, threat of, 234–5

superintendent of schools, 200–2

sympathy, basis for, 150

T

taxpayers, 146

tax preparers, failures by, 78–80

tax refund, erroneous, 142–4

tax returns, joint, signatures for, 144

telephone calls:
  harassing, 182–3
  unreturned, 95–7

Tennessee:
  Commerce and Insurance Department, 294
  Consumer Affairs Division, 271, 320
  Consumer Protection Division, 271
  Education Department, 311
  Financial Institutions Department, 303
  small claims courts in, 255
  Transportation Department, 328

testing, medical, *see* medical testing

Texas:
  Banking Department, 303
  Consumer Protection Division, 271–2, 320
  Education Agency, 311
  Insurance Department, 285, 294

Public Insurance Counsel, Office of, 272

small claims courts in, 255–6

Transportation Department, 328

third parties, 60, 173, 191

time payments:
  crediting of, 172–3
  problems with, 173

tone, appropriate, 10, 29, 132, 192, 194

traffic court, judge or clerk of, 150–3

traffic department, state, stoplight installation requested, 147–9

transportation agencies, state, 323–328

TransUnion, LLC, 329

travel, 219–31

travel agents, misleading information from, 219–20

trucking companies, furniture damaged by, 69–70

U

unbundling, 122

unjustified claims, by collection agencies and lawyers, 184–6

unpaid balances, 167

unpaid bills, 189–90

unpaid debts, 191–2

used cars, return of, 57–8

Utah:
  Consumer Protection Division, 272
  Education Office, 311
  Financial Institutions Department, 303, 320
  Insurance Department, 286, 294
  small claims courts in, 256
  Transportation Department, 328

utility companies, inadequate service by, 93–4

V

Vermont:
  Banking, Insurance, Securities and Health Care Administration, 303
  Consumer Assistance Program for Consumer Complaints and Questions, 272, 320
  Consumer Assurance Section, Food and Market, 272
  Education Department, 311
  Health Care Administration, 286
  Insurance Division, 294
  Public Protection Division, 272
  small claims courts in, 256

Transportation Agency, 328

Virginia:
Attorney General, 273
Consumer Affairs Office, 272, 320
Education Department, 311
Financial Institutions Bureau, 303
Insurance Bureau, Office of Managed Care, 286
small claims courts in, 256
State Corporation Commission, 294
Transportation Department, 328

W

warranty, 245
breach of, 54
claims on, 54–6
manufacturer's, 46

Washington:
Consumer Resource Center, 273, 320–1
Financial Institutions Department, 303
Health Department, 286
Insurance Commissioner, 295

Office of Superintendent of Public Instruction, 311
small claims courts in, 256
Transportation Department, 328

West Virginia:
Banking Division, 304
Consumer Protection Division, 273, 321
Education Department, 312
Insurance Department, 295
small claims courts in, 257
Transportation Department, 328
Weights and Measures Section, 273

wheelchair accessibility, 209–10

Wisconsin:
Financial Institutions Department, 304
Insurance Commissioner, 295
Public Instruction Department, 312
small claims courts in, 257

Trade and Consumer Protection Department, 274, 321–2
Transportation Department, 328

witnesses, 60, 77

work:
defective, 63, 64, 81–2
faulty, 62–4
money owed for, 189–90

"workmanlike fashion," 24, 85

written records, see documents, documentation

"wrongful denial," 23, 24

Wyoming:
Attorney General's Office, 274
Consumer Protection Unit, 274, 322
Division of Banking, 304
Education Department, 312
Insurance Department, 295
small claims courts in, 257
Transportation Department, 328